Science and the
Early Adolescent

Compiled by

Michael J. Padilla
Department of Science Education
University of Georgia
Athens, Georgia 30602

National Science Teachers Association

Acknowledgements

The National Science Teachers Association is deeply indebted to the number of individuals and associations who have permitted us to reprint their work here. Each author and publisher is credited in the table of contents along with the corresponding article, but we wish to extend a special thanks right at the outset for the cooperation that made this volume possible.

Some of the illustrations in the book were taken from the original articles, but additional art was required as the articles were reformatted for the book. Graduate student Lydia Nolan-Davis of The University of Georgia at Athens worked with the volume compiler to conceive the illustrations appearing here. NSTA thanks Ms. Nolan-Davis for applying her artistic talent so generously to the subject of science education and would like to announce that she is available for commission by writing The University of Georgia Department of Science Education in Athens, GA 30602.

Finally, NSTA would like to commend and thank the committed panel of reviewers who worked with this compilation from the beginning. The core group involved in the project consists of the compiler, Michael J. Padilla, from the The University of Georgia at Athens; Nancy C. Griffin from The University of Florida at Gainesville; Robert Kilburn from The Public Schools of Newton, Massachusetts; Karen E. Reynolds from The University of California at Berkeley; Terry Shaw from Kansas State University at Manhattan; and Michael J. Wavering from the Model Laboratory School at Eastern Kentucky University in Richmond.

Sources of quotations appearing on the section dividers throughout the book follow:

INTRODUCTION
Judson, Horace. *The Search for Solutions*. NY: Holt, Rinehart and Winston, 1980.
Hurd, Paul DeHart, et al. *The Status of Middle School and Junior High School Science*. Louisville, CO: Center for Educational Research and Evaluation Report, 31 December 1981.

DEVELOPMENTAL CHARACTERISTICS OF THE EARLY ADOLESCENT
Hurd, Paul DeHart, et al. *Op cit*.

TEACHING STRATEGIES
Farmer, Walter and Margaret Farrell. *Systematic Instruction in Science for the Middle and High School Years*. Reading, MA: Addison-Wesley Publishing Co., 1980.
Hurd, Paul DeHart, et al. *Op cit*.
Schwebel, Milton and Jane Raph. *Piaget in the Classroom*. NY: Basic Books, Inc., 1973.

ACTIVITIES
Science and Mathematics in the Schools: Report of a Convocation. DC: National Academy Press, 1982.
Hurd, Paul DeHart, et al. *Op cit*.
Kamii, Constance. *Piaget in the Classroom*. NY: Basic Books, Inc., 1973.

Preface

By any definition middle and junior high school science education have come a long way in a relatively short time. A strong drive to reorganize the middle level of our educational system began in the late sixties in response to teacher and parent dissatisfaction with the status of the junior high school at the time. The institution had become no more than a little high school, disregarding its role as a transitional unit between elementary and high school. Not all junior high schools changed their names to middle school, but many, if not most, reevaluated their role in the educational system. This focus on the middle level of education and the students at this level instigated a companion emphasis on early adolescence in science education.

When the National Science Teachers Association established a middle/junior high school division in its 1975 reorganization, the status of teaching science to early adolescents was elevated considerably. Subsequent work by division leaders and committee members focused attention on problems associated with teaching science to 10–15 year olds. *The Middle/Junior High Science Bulletin*, a direct outgrowth of the division's work, was first published in February 1978 and continues with a new name, *Science Scope*, today. In recent years, both *Science and Children* and *The Science Teacher* have increased their emphasis on science teaching at the middle school level through more and better articles and particularly through *Science and Children*'s regularly appearing column, "Early Adolescence." During this same period the National Science Foundation dedicated several grants to improving science and mathematics education in junior high and middle schools. Even though this source of funding has recently been eliminated, the fruits of projects begun in the late 1970s are now being borne.

One outgrowth of some of these projects is research which points to the middle school years as a time during which an individual's future in science education is shaped. An awareness of the shortcomings of science education at this level has coupled with a renewed interest in the special needs and problems of students at this level to spur an unprecedented degree of curricular and organizational change.

In a recent report entitled, *The Status of Middle School and Junior High School Science*, Paul Hurd and his colleagues survey science education practices, materials, and research related to the early adolescent. The study, funded by the National Science Foundation, was intended to determine the status of science teaching and "to propose recommendations and prospectives for improving science education at these grade levels for the eighties and beyond." While the entire report is important reading, the recommendations are most relevant here. The authors state:

> Science instruction needs to reflect the way scientific knowledge is created and grows, its relationship and role in our technological society, and its limitations as a way of knowing. Thus, the instruction should involve students in problematic contexts, in making choices, considering options, contemplating risks, analyzing alternatives, and developing respect for varying points of view based on different interpretations of valid data.

Later they continue:

> . . . knowledge acquistion is not the only end goal of science schooling. Utilization of knowledge in a problem context requires the intellectual skills of organizing information, analytical and deductive reasoning, problem identification, problem solving, risk assessment, value identification, and much more.

This is the philosophy that *Science and the Early Adolescent* expresses.

Science and the Early Adolescent gathers together selections from recent writing, thinking, and speaking about middle and junior high school science. Several journals are represented here, including *The Middle/Junior High Science Bulletin*, *Science and Children*, *The Science Teacher*, *The Middle School Journal*, *School Science and Mathematics*, and *Childhood Education*. Every article that might be appropriate for the middle school or junior high school science teacher was reviewed and the best chosen for inclusion. Every effort was made to communicate a coherent message to the teacher. That message—that the early adolescent is unique and deserves a unique experience in science, one different from both elementary and secondary science—recurs in many articles.

The introduction to *Science and the Early Adolescent* gives a philosophical backdrop to teaching in the middle or junior high school, addressing questions about the special demands of teaching at this level. For those unfamiliar with the unique developmental characteristics of the early adolescent, the second section gives a bit of background and emphasizes the cognitive and social/emotional aspects of this development. The third section presents articles that focus on the methodology of teaching science. Several concentrate on the difficult aspects of teaching 10–15 year olds and discuss topics like managing the classroom, organizing the laboratory, assessing a science program, and generally utilizing a variety of teaching resources and methods. The last section gives examples of some very creative and often overlooked answers to the "what to teach" question. Sample activities or unit ideas from the life and physical sciences, many stressing scientific thinking or science process skills, are featured.

No book can satisfy all the needs of middle and junior high school science teachers. This long neglected group can, however, reasonably expect that attention will once again be focused on their students and that the difficulty, as well as the necessity, of teaching science at the middle level will be acknowledged. The intent of this book is to help bring these particular concerns into focus. I hope you will agree that it accomplishes this goal.

Michael J. Padilla

Contents

ACTIVITIES

Introduction

Science has several rewards, but the greatest is that it is the most interesting, difficult, pitiless, exciting and beautiful pursuit that we have yet found. Science is our century's art.

Horace Judson
The Search for Solutions

. . . early adolescence is a crucial time for:
- Forming attitudes about self in relation to schooling
- Forming attitudes about self in relation to science
- Forming attitudes about self in relation to technology
- Acquiring essential skills of reading scientific materials, written and oral expression, research, and investigation basic to further effective knowledge acquisition and utilization.

Therefore, teachers should be given support in learning how best to facilitate the development of these attitudes and skills.

Paul DeHart Hurd, et al.
The Status of Middle School and
Junior High School Science

Middle School/Junior High Science: Changing Perspectives

Paul DeHart Hurd

In our schools, early adolescents form a very special group of students. But, they are not always viewed in terms of their uniqueness. Until recently sociologists, psychologists, and educators focused much of their research on early childhood and adolescent development, neglecting the life span between these two phases of maturation. Sporadically, the middle group is included in educational surveys to be sure they are still there, but not much seems to happen in knowing more about them. Several years ago in a study on the early adolescent and the learning of science, prepared for the National Science Foundation, I commented: "Unrecognized, underprivileged, and undereducated describe the early adolescent in the American school system."(1)*

SOME POSITIVE RESULTS

In spite of all the social turmoil in America and undue pressures on schools there are worthwhile developments. The concept of the middle school has evolved stressing the importance of a separate school environment for 10- to 14-year-olds. In 1977, the National Science Teachers Association formed a middle school/junior high section to promote effective science teaching. The same year, the Science Education Directorate of the National Science Foundation made science education of early adolescents a focus of interest. Also, a national Center for Early Adolescence was established at the University of North Carolina.(2) The *1981 Yearbook* of the Association for the Education of Teachers of Science is devoted exclusively to middle school science.(3) From all of these efforts, an increasing number of concerned teachers and administrators are devising ways to revitalize science teaching for early adolescents.

A NEED FOR PERSPECTIVES

What has not clearly emerged in the history of the middle school is a conceptual framework or rationale to justify and guide the teaching of science. Educational innovation has been largely limited to organizational and administrative matters with a minimum of curriculum development. Of primary importance is the identification of goals and policies that: 1) are consistent with the current nature of the scientific and technological enterprises; 2) harmonize with recent cultural shifts in American life; and 3) recognize fully the uniqueness of the early adolescent as an individual and as a member of society. Without such a base, for debate and action, our most well intentioned teaching efforts may be little more than frivolous activities.

---

*See References and Notes.

THE SEARCH BEGINS

In 1980, with financial support from the National Science Foundation (NSF), a research team operating under the aegis of the Center for Educational Research and Evaluation (CERE) began a fifteen month study of science teaching in the middle schools.(4) The team analyzed previously reported national surveys of science teaching completed between 1965-1970 and 1975-1980. The purpose in using the two time periods was to detect whether cultural shifts and changes in the enterprises of science and technology over the past decade are reflected in the middle school curriculum. The team searched especially for the rationale, goals, and objectives which seemed to represent the conceptual basis for middle school science teaching. Among the findings was the discovery that less than half of the middle schools in the United States have a science program designed specifically for the purpose of improving educational opportunities for early adolescents.

A fundamental question is what do scientists, and science curriculum developers each think middle school science teaching should be about? The team could not find a commonly accepted set of purposes, nor a theoretical or empirical justification for what was being taught. It did learn that a majority of middle school science teachers found the following instructional objectives to be unacceptable: 1) development of inquiry skills; 2) scientific literacy; 3) career awareness; 4) science/technology/society interactions; 5) ethical and value implications of science and technology; 6) science for effective citizenship; 7) appreciation of science and 8) understanding one's self and the world in which we live. Such goals were regarded as diffuse, impractical, remote, unrealistic, and sometimes contrary to community beliefs.

A LOOK AT TEXTBOOKS

Knowing that textbooks largely determine what is taught in schools, the CERE team did a content analysis of commonly used science textbooks for the middle grades.

Of twenty innovative science programs proposed, or under development, for middle schools in the late 1960s, only one, the Intermediate Science Curriculum Study, has made it into the list of twelve top-selling programs ten years later. There were only minimal differences between an edition of a textbook published in the 1960s and an edition of the same book published in the late 1970s or 1980s. In the textbook analysis, the team discovered middle school science texts that introduced as many as 2,500 technical terms and unfamiliar words per single book. A beginning foreign language course requires half this number of new words. Today, the vocabulary load of most middle school science textbooks is so great that it essentially precludes a conceptualization of scientific ideas and principles.

STUDENT OPINIONS OF SCIENCE

Information obtained from the three National Assessments of Educational Progress (NAEP) in the sciences indicated student attitudes toward science and about science teaching. Some student reactions were these: 1) They are lukewarm about their science courses; 2) They like English and mathematics better; 3) They feel science is interesting, and teachers try hard to make the subject exciting; and

4) They do not feel competent in learning science because there are too many facts to memorize. The peak level of student interest in science between kindergarten and high school graduation occurs during the middle school years, yet two-thirds of the Middle School students state they would not take another course in science unless required to do so.

One of the more intriguing findings from the NAEP data shows that the level of middle school student understanding of the interrelation of science, technology, and society exceeds the amount of such information found in the textbooks they use. By age thirteen, most students are at about the same level of scientific literacy as their parents.

PROFESSIONAL GROWTH

Middle/jr. high science teachers get most of their professional information from other teachers who have attended regional or national conventions, book salesmen, or college courses. Educational theory, the results of research in science teaching, and college-based science teaching specialists are viewed with suspicion and judged to have little to offer for correcting educational deficiencies. Professional journals such as *The Science Teacher* and *Science and Children*, are perceived by half of the middle school teachers to be their best source of information on science teaching, yet nearly two-thirds of middle school science teachers admit they do not read professional journals.

THE MIDDLE SCHOOL CONCEPT

The philosophical concepts behind the middle school movement were studied. From the time the junior high school was organized early in this century, there has been almost continuous debate about its legitimacy as a separate part of the educational system. Criticism of this "stepchild of public education" reached a critical high point early in the 1960s. As an alternative to the junior high, a middle school concept evolved representing a rethinking of what an educational program for early adolescents should be like. This debate is still going on. There is a consensus that 10- to 14-year-olds have special physical, cognitive, affective, and social needs. There is also agreement that many of these needs have become intensified in recent years, reflecting changes in family life styles, changes in social living, and new demands upon the adaptive capacities of young people.

NEW SCIENCE TEACHING PERSPECTIVES EMERGE

The CERE team studied 30 commission reports on science education published since 1970. The team's interpretation of the reports formed the basis for the following perspectives on teaching science in the 1980s.

1. Science and technology have become fused in their impact on society and personal affairs. This suggests, a) that science and technology both have a place in the school science curriculum, and b) that a social context for science teaching is a priority in new curriculum developments.

2. Science and technology in a social context invariably raise value and ethical questions both personal and social. These issues are not to be avoided in science teaching since they cannot be avoided in real life.

3. A primary concern in all teaching is the acquisition of knowledge. Of equal importance is how knowledge can be utilized effectively. This means science teaching should be extended to include the skills essential to the processing of scientific and technological information for personal and social use.

4. The effective utilization of scientific information in human affairs requires that a student have an understanding of, a) how to make decisions by selecting actions among alternatives; b) what risk means; and c) how preferences, ethics, and values influence judgment.

5. To properly display the interaction of science, technology, and society requires that a major fraction of science courses be organized in terms of problems, some societal others personal. Typical of these problems would be health, energy, human growth and development, management of natural resources, and the leisure uses of science among others.

6. Science courses should include problems that students will need to deal with throughout their lifetime. This suggests a science curriculum more oriented to the future than to the present or past. For many years, the tone of instruction in science courses has been largely oriented toward the past and taught as a history. How often have we heard "this is what scientists have learned" as though science were a closed book? The basic assumption underlying a future perspective for science teaching is that neither science, technology, nor society is static. The only constant in all of life is change. Now that human beings are in control of their own evolution through the problems they generate or resolve, our future well-being can be jeopardized by courses in science and technology that have only historical meaning.

We are in the midst of both a social and scientific revolution and herein lies our professional challenge, a science program that at least parallels these changes.

REFERENCES AND NOTES

1. Hurd, Paul DeHart (Ed.). *Early Adolescents: Perspectives and Recommendations*. Prepared for the National Science Foundation, Directorate for Science Education. Washington, D.C. U.S. Government Printing Office. 1978.
2. Center for Early Adolescence. Suite 223, Carr Mill Mall, Carrboro, N.C. 27510.
3. Ochs, V. Daniel (Ed.). *1981 AETS Yearbook: Improving Practices in Middle School Science*. ERIC/SMEAC Reference Center, The Ohio State University, 1200 Chambers Road—3rd Floor, Columbus, Ohio 43212.
4. Center for Educational Research and Evaluation*. A Continuing Program of the BSCS, Louisville, CO. Members of the research team were: Principal Investigators: Paul DeHart Hurd and James T. Robinson. Research Associates: Mary C. McConnell and Norris M. Ross, Jr.

*Note: Copies of the CERE Report are available from BSCS, 833 W. South Boulder Road, Louisville, CO 80027.

Junior to What?

Donna DeSeyn

And they called it the junior high school!

There's something about being junior that suggests immaturity. Was the junior high so named to condemn it to eternal immaturity?

What can its future be? It can never grow up and become senior high school, for to do so would leave a void in the system at one of the most critical stages of student development. So it goes on forever as junior.

Junior to what? To senior, of course. Junior learns to emulate senior—to walk like him, talk like him, think like him—until someday he replaces him. Is that what is supposed to happen to the junior high school? Is it supposed to emulate the senior high school—to behave like it, to schedule like it, to test like it, to emphasize content like it? If so, it is well named. But if not . . .

The junior high school is far more than a little high school. Its students have different needs, its teachers different aspirations for their students. Junior high students are students in transition. They are at a point in their lives where they are no longer children, but not yet adults. Nevertheless, their intellectual, emotional, and social needs are just as distinctive. They are very much aware, for example, of their changing bodies; are vulnerable to peer pressure; would like to assert a bit of self-independence, but are still very much in need of parental guidance; are reaching a crucial stage in the development of their intellectual self-image. Such needs and pressures can no longer be satisfied by the elementary school approach; yet to diminish the importance of this transitional stage by saying that it must conform to the way the senior high does things means that our junior high students are in for a disastrous three years of self-deception.

Early adolescents must have experiences which wean them from the protective care of the mother/father image of the elementary teacher and help them grow to deal with a variety of adults. They must learn to move from a child-centered experience to a content-centered experience. To expect such a change to occur by giving them a summer vacation to grow up, or even by breaking them into seventh grade gently during the first quarter, is to wish for miracles.

Many school experiences which should occur at the early adolescent stage have been identified. They can be provided by the public schools and provided well. But, they must be provided by a mature program, and I'm not sure that the "junior" high school mentality is able to provide it. The junior high school must grow up for this to happen, and it can't happen as long as it thinks of itself as "junior."

Objectives for Middle School Science

Burton E. Voss

Middle school science is an important topic which is currently being emphasized by local school districts and national government agencies alike. One reason for this emphasis is the alarming evidence that 50 percent of all students take no more science after high school biology, typically a first year high school course. This fact has real implications for science taught in the middle school, yet the question, "What should middle school science be?" is not a simple one. This article attempts to outline some of the issues involved in answering it.

CONCEPT DEVELOPMENT

The middle school student is still learning facts, but is beginning to assimilate and integrate them into concepts and conceptual frameworks, depending on the stage of his/her intellectual development. Of particular importance, the students should be learning how applications of basic concepts are of use in understanding and solving problems involving health, energy, environmental pollution, and technology. These man-made problems could be studied as separate units or infused into the regular curriculum.

Examples of concepts middle school students should study are:

Life Science: environment, life cycle, habitat, population, ecosystem, circulation, respiration, digestion, excretion, reproduction, photosynthesis, succession, recycle, behavior, classification, heredity, adaptation.

Earth Sciences: seasons, erosion, weather, fossil record, eclipse, humidity, weather front, air pressure, water cycle, earth's crust, mineral, space exploration, orbital motion, precipitation, continental drift, solar system, gravity, sediment, weathering, geologic time scale, solar energy.

Physical Sciences: property, density, boiling point, model, magnetic field, electric current, circuit, electromagnet, force, matter, element, interactions, solution, buoyancy, energy transformation, light, sound, doubling time, net energy, nuclear energy, machine.

PROCESSES OF SCIENCE

In the middle school, process skills should be developed to foster decision making. As the child progresses through the lower grades, the basic processes are developed: observing, inferring; using space/time relationships; measuring; communicating; classifying and predicting. In the middle school years integrative processes should be developed such as: formulation-hypotheses; identifying and controlling variables; interpreting data; and experimenting. Eventually all of these skills should be

Art by Lydia Nolan-Davis

synthesized into problem solving where students can: identify a problem; state a hypothesis; gather relevant data; study alternatives; interpret the data; make a decision based on the data; gain ideas for new research. Students should be afforded the opportunity to use problem solving related to issues in science, technology and society.

Closely related to the processes of science are psychomotor and investigative skills—primarily laboratory based. Science programs place special emphasis upon these skills and it is for this reason they are recommended. These skills are:

1. The use of laboratory equipment such as the Bunsen burner, balances, thermometers, volume measurements, and the microscope.
2. The use of library references, scientific figures, scientific notation, the metric system, writing laboratory reports, and communicating data.

NATURE OF SCIENCE, SCIENTISTS, AND SOCIAL IMPLICATIONS

The middle school science program should include opportunities for systematic instruction related to the nature of science, scientists, and technology. First of all, students should understand that science is for everyone, regardless of race, sex, physical or mental handicaps. They should recognize there are multidisciplinary aspects to science with implications that societal problems cannot be solved by science alone. Also, science is a human enterprise—it involves laws, values and moral decisions. Students should be sensitized to the abuses of science and technology. They also need to understand that science is open ended and revisionary. They need to understand scientists, their values, and the methods they use.

Recent studies by the National Assessment of Educational Progress(2) indicate that 46 percent of 13 year olds tested feel that science has caused *most* or *some* of today's problems. On the other hand, 58 percent of the 13 year olds feel that science will solve *most* of the nation's problems. There are concerns about how science alone can solve problems. More and more science discoveries and technology have societal impacts; for example, environmental effects of nuclear power reactors and coal fired plants. Student attitudes and their moral reasoning can be aided by integrating science and social studies. Through integrated programs, students can learn the importance of science, science and social science, scientists, and the scientific methods needed to solve human problems.

PERSONAL-SOCIAL GOALS

The middle school years are the times when students need assistance with the development of personal-social goals. The students are acutely aware of themselves: how they look; how they dress; and their relationships with their peers. The *Report on Early Adolescence* states "the early adolescent is newly awakened to the imperfection and hypocrisy of the adult world."(3) They wonder what the world has in store for them. The study of careers in science and technology should be a part of the curriculum. The concept that *variability* in height, weight, sexual development, intelligence, and cognition development is *normal* should be stressed. Students should observe that teachers care for them and counsel them. The "small house" arrangement where a cluster of 100 students is served by a curriculum team, plus house counselor, is an interesting innovation in some middle schools. The middle school is a place where social skills can be developed and a place where extremely deviant behavior should not be tolerated.

REMEDIAL SKILL DEVELOPMENT AND ENRICHMENT

Lastly, provisions for diagnostic testing to determine basic skills in reading and mathematics should be made. The data are very clear that many students are below grade levels in basic math and reading skill development. Students should have the opportunity for *remediation or enrichment* of reading and mathematics skills. Epstein(4) has found from his research that there is little gain in the size of the brain in children between 12 and 14. He implies that little intellectual development occurs at that time. Thus he is much in favor of the concept of remediation and exploratory enrichment in the middle school. A good middle school program should provide activities such as school camping or outdoor education activities, visits to museums, visits to scientific and technological laboratories, a science club or an ecology club for all students. In addition, many schools have a program for the gifted.

CONCLUSION

Objectives for middle school science should recognize the physical and intellectual development of students. Knowledge and problem solving are important tools for investigating and understanding science-societal issues. Integration of mathematics skills, science objectives, and social science objectives should be implemented. Development of creative curricula to assist early adolescents to cope in a scientific and technological world are a real challenge to middle school educators.

BIBLIOGRAPHY

1. National Science Foundation, 1978, *Early Adolescence, Perspectives and Recommendations*. Superintendent of Documents, U.S. Government Printing Office, Washington, D.C., p. 58.
2. National Assessment of Educational Progress, Dec., 1979. *Newsletter*, Vol. XII, No. 6, p. 1.
3. Ibid., *Early Adolescence*.
4. Epstein, H. and Toeffer, C., 1978, "A Neuro-Science Basis for Reorganizing Middle School Science", *Educational Leadership*, May, pp. 656-660.

OTHER REFERENCES

1. George, Paul S. Editor. *The Middle School—A Look Ahead*. National Middle School Association, University of Florida, Gainsville, FL., 1978.
2. "Human Sciences for the Middle School", reprint from *BSCS Newsletter #44*, BSCS, P.O. Box 930, Boulder, CO 80302.
3. Kohlberg, Lawrence. Moral Education and Research Foundation, Harvard Graduate School of Education, Roy E. Larsen Hall, Appian Way, Cambridge, Massachusetts 02138.
4. Michigan Association of Middle School Educators, 1974. *Position Statement*, Michigan Junior High-Middle School Task Force. Robert Hall, Secondary School Principals Association, Bureau of School Services, University of Michigan, 401 S. Fourth Street, Ann Arbor, MI 48109.
5. Minnesota Department of Education. *Essential Learner Outcomes in Science*. St. Paul, Minnesota.
6. Minnesota Department of Education. 1976. Minnesota Middle School Profile. St. Paul, Minnesota.
7. Stock, R. and Hansen, Lee. 1979. *Revised Proposals for Modifying the Intermediate Science Program*. Ann Arbor Public Schools, 2555 South State Street, Ann Arbor, Michigan 48105.
8. *The Status of Pre-College Science, Mathematics, and Social Science Education: 1955-1975*. Volume 1, Science Education. Superintendent of Documents, U.S. Government Printing Office, Washington, D.C. 20402. Price: $4.25.

A Not So Tongue in Cheek View of Middle School Classrooms

Dorothy Rathbun [Kennedy]

So you've taken on the job of teaching science to a bunch of middle schoolers, eh? Congratulations are in order—(1) for your good fortune in finding (or keeping) a job in today's glutted market, and (2) for your courage. You will need every ounce of courage you can muster, for today's middle schoolers are not exactly what some of us oldtimers used to call "nice, well-behaved children." They can be such demons, in fact, that given a choice, you might choose to walk into a den of lions rather than your fifth period class.

Maybe rule No. 1 should be: Don't turn your back on your students—especially if you have Bunsen burners or dissecting kits at hand. Forget about writing on the blackboard. Rig up an overhead projector so you can face the class as you jot down notes and assignments for them to copy off the wall or screen behind you. You'll find other advantages to overheads too. You can prepare (or buy) your transparencies ahead of time, and you can use all kinds of fancy overlays.

Many veteran teachers swear that middle school children are the toughest audience in the world. Avid TV-viewers from birth, they have absorbed everything from "Sesame Street" to "Baretta," and when they come to school, what they want most is to be entertained. You can deplore that tendency all you want, but you need to face the truth of it.

If you have any dramatic talent, don't fight it. Let it have full sway in your classroom. Studying bacteria? Come in dressed as Louis Pasteur. Reptiles? Drape a snake around your neck. The moon? Rent a space-man suit. It's not absolutely essential to be an entertainer, but you must at least acknowledge the need for variety in your classroom. You probably were attracted to the field of science in the first place because you found it exciting, fascinating, thrilling, filled with incredible bits and pieces of information that turned you on. How can you help your students learn to see the world of science in the same way? You can't do it by lecturing every day or giving long reading assignments with questions to answer at the end of the chapter. Students this age literally won't sit still for it.

If you're going to work with middle school students, let this thought be engraved on your brain: They have a short attention span and an incredibly high energy level. That's why they squirm so much when you do all the talking. Try to find some games or activities that will let them get up and move around the room once in a while. Keep in mind, though, that they're clumsy, like puppies that haven't grown up to fit their feet yet. So don't leave a rack of test tubes in the middle of the floor. Use movies, filmstrips, videotapes, displays and exhibits, individual and group projects, study guides, workbooks, puzzles, student demonstrations, drills, pop quizzes—whatever it takes to keep things lively and moving.

While you want lively activity, of course, what you do *not* want is destructiveness and danger. So you will have to establish in the beginning that you are the boss. You are not their pal or their playmate. You are their host, and as long as they behave like ladies and gentlemen (or reasonable facsimiles, as such matters go in 1978), they are welcome guests in your laboratory. You have a lot of interesting objects for them to look at and experiments for them to conduct, but they must obey a few simple ground rules without question or argument. You convince them of all this through sheer force of personality. You have to say what you mean, say it clearly, and make it stick. A science classroom can't be run reasonably any other way. Let them know the ground rules the first day. Then get on with all those exciting projects.

Science teachers as a group tend to be fairly well organized and tidy people. Unfortunately, middle school students as a group do not. Your youngest students are apt to have a terrible time just getting their bodies, notebooks, pencils, and textbooks all into the classroom at the same time. Be patient with them at first, but make it clear that this is a minimum daily requirement. Then you can move on to bigger and better tasks, like helping them improve their study habits. Let them know that standard cop-outs like "you know what I mean" and "that's close enough" are not acceptable in your classroom. Insist on proper terminology, correctly spelled, forming exact and accurate answers.

It's hardly popular in educational circles today to speak of rote memorization, but let's be brave enough to admit that basic science courses require this skill. Show your students how to memorize a list of terms. Tell them to say the word and the definition, then cover up the definition, say the word, and try to supply the meaning without peeking. Then do it in reverse. Pair students off for this exercise. Walk around the room and listen. Shoot rapid-fire questions at them.

Of course, you're after more than good memory skills and high quiz scores. You want your students to grasp some broader concepts about the very things that excited you about science in the first place. If you can get through the basics with them successfully, you have a good chance of helping them cross over into this wondrous area. Your own enthusiasm will be the key and someday it will all fall into place. You may not hear a click when that happens. But you could very well (over) hear a hallway comment like, "I can hardly wait for science class today." And when you can hardly wait to get to school yourself, then you'll know you've really arrived. The demons are no longer demons, and the work is beginning to resemble fun. Congratulations! Your bravery and determination have paid off.

Developmental Characteristics of the Early Adolescent

Early adolescents, 11 to 14 year olds,
are more varied physically,
intellectually, and socially than any
other school age group. The extent
of these variations suggests that the
goals and subject matter of science
education should be special for this
age group. Such a science education
program would take into
consideration the intellectual and
social needs of these young people as
they progress toward adulthood.

Paul DeHart Hurd, et al.
*The Status of Middle School and
Junior High School Science*

Formal Operations and Middle/Junior High School Science Education

Michael J. Padilla

"If Piaget's notions are correct, then much of the time spent on science instruction in elementary and middle schools today is wasted. Even worse, if we continue to insist that students learn ideas that they are unable to understand because they lack the logical structures necessary for understanding, they have little choice but to resort to rote memory. As a result, they develop poor study habits, poor attitudes toward school and low self image." (4)

The impact of Jean Piaget's writings on education has been considerable. Science education in particular has felt the influence of Piaget through the general philosophy which promotes a "hands-on" approach to science as well as programs such as the Science Curriculum Improvement Study (15) and Science 5/13 (14) which are based on Piagetian theory. In the last few years, a relatively large and controversial body of literature regarding science teaching and cognitive development has emerged. What effects could or should this research have on the classroom teacher of grades six through nine?

DEVELOPMENT REVIEWED

Piaget and his co-workers defined four basic, sequential stages in the development of logical thinking abilities. (12) According to Piaget's writings, the concrete and formal operational stages are of greatest concern to the children and teachers of grades six through nine because most children of these ages (11-14) can be classified in one of them or in transition.

Most important to understanding what Piaget really meant by concrete and formal operations is a knowledge of his goals and methods. He made generalizations about the cognitive structures or network of operations that a child had available for solving logical problems. Obviously, one cannot simply measure these structures, but rather must infer their existence through physical and verbal responses to problem situations. These responses are the heart of the clinical method, developed by Piaget, in which the child is asked to justify his solution orally. Thus, one often hears references made about students' abilities with tasks. What must be remembered is that the basis for success on a properly administered task is the cognitive structures available to the student.

While there is some disagreement as to what actually constitutes formal thought processes (7), several standard tasks developed by Piaget have been used extensively. These tasks are problem oriented and usually challenge a subject's ability to identify and control variables, to use proportional thought, to apply propositional logic, and/or to use a combination of reasoning abilities.

RESEARCH FINDINGS ON FORMAL OPERATIONS

Starting with Lovell's studies in 1961, evidence began accumulating that not all children move from concrete to formal operations at age 11 or 12 as Piaget asserted. In fact, a great discrepancy between research findings and theory has become evident. Many college freshmen have even been found predominantly using concrete thought processes. Chiapetta concluded from several formal operational studies that most (over 85%) adolescents and young adults have not fully developed formal operational abilities. (2) In 1978, Renner tested almost 600 students from grades 7-12 administering six tasks to each student. Only 17% of the seventh graders, 23% of the eighth graders and 34% of the twelfth graders exhibited formal thought processes. (13) While other research studies (5,6) show slightly different numbers of subjects at formal operational levels, the overall generalization that can be drawn is that most children in middle and junior high schools cannot use abstract reasoning abilities.

CONCRETE AND FORMAL CONCEPTS

Lawson and Renner (8) divided selected science content into either concrete concepts (those that can be developed with firsthand experience with objects) or formal concepts (those whose meaning is derived through the theoretical models of science, not from concrete objects). Digestion and bulb brightness are examples of concrete concepts; ecosystems and nuclear energy are formal concepts. After the regular classroom teacher taught a unit, the students were tested for understanding of the material. For the purposes of this study, understanding was defined as the ability to answer content questions at comprehension and application levels using Bloom's taxonomy. Across all subject areas, formal thinkers performed considerably higher than concrete thinkers. Especially interesting, however, is the fact that almost no concrete thinking students showed mastery of formal concepts. While formal thinking students did master some formal concepts, they performed much higher on the concrete concepts.

Following up on these results, Cantu and Herron (1) explored the relative efficiency of using illustrations, diagrams and models to teach formal and concrete students. They concluded that no matter what kind of concepts were being taught that formal students understood better than concrete students, that concrete students did not learn any of the formal concepts very well and that concrete students did learn concrete concepts provided that formal reasoning was not part of the teaching strategy used. Similarly Goodstein and Howe attempted to show that concrete models and exemplars encourage better understanding by both concrete and formal learners. (3)

Although these studies were conducted with high school students and high school subject matter, it is likely that similar results would occur with children aged 10-14. Certainly the data from these studies implies that science teachers at all grade levels should be taking a long, hard look at their course content. If a great number of students are not formally operational, even by grade twelve, and if concrete operational students do not learn formal concepts, then middle/junior high school teachers should both concentrate on concrete concepts instead of the more abstract ideas of science and should attempt to develop teaching procedures that use concrete examples, models and other materials as much as possible.

TEACHING AND DEVELOPMENT

Should teachers only reduce the complexity of science content and not attempt to raise the level of thought among students? No, teachers should continue to identify successful teaching strategies and to apply them in the classroom. In a review of recent literature, Levine and Linn listed several variables relevant to scientific or formal reasoning. Among these are the number of variables in a given problem, the students' familiarity with the variables, the amount and quality of school experience, the strategy for task completion and the students' problem-organization skills. (9) All of the above factors can be somewhat controlled by the classroom teacher. By organizing numerous experiences with experimental variables and situations with which children are familiar and by carefully controlling the number and complexity of the variables being considered, the teacher can begin to shape the experiential background of students. Also, teachers can present useful learning strategies, ones which help to solve types of problems (e.g., an emphasis on a "fair" experiment) and ones which help to organize and clarify information (written records and charts).

These generalizations were made from numerous individual and independent studies. None of these studies was greatly successful at improving the level of thought as measured by transfer of abilities on highly related tasks. But most used only short term training sessions. While long-term effects of such procedures can only be conjecture at this time, these methods offer good possibilities.

SUMMARY

These research results point to several conclusions for middle/junior high school teachers. Most children aged 10-14 are not formally operational and no matter how teachers teach, the students will have great difficulty comprehending abstract science concepts. Teachers should review curriculum topics and cull out the unnecessary abstract concepts. Contrary to high school science where formal concepts are intrinsic to chemistry and physics instruction, there is no real curricular necessity for teaching abstractions to children in grades six to nine. Enough important concrete concepts are available.

One final note of importance to science teachers is that over the past twenty years, much emphasis has been placed on the science process skills. This dimension arose out of the curriculum development projects of the 50's and 60's. Of enormous importance is the similarity between the process skills and many of Piaget's logical abilities, such as identifying and controlling variables, hypothesizing, application of proportional reasoning in data interpretation activities, classification, describing relationships and many others. (11) Thus, when trying to enhance development through science teaching, no new philosophy of teaching need be adopted. The classroom teacher should continue to use concrete activities stressing appropriate process skills. The only new awareness is that many of the process skill abilities are developmental in nature and thus will not and usually cannot be learned over a short period of time.

REFERENCES

1. Cantu, L., and Herron, D. "Concrete and Formal Piagetian Stages and Science Concepts Attainment." Journal of Research in Science Teaching, 15: 135-143; March 1978.
2. Chiapetta, E. "A Review of Piagetian Studies Relevant to Science Instruction at the Secondary and College Level." Science Education, 60:253-261; April-June 1976.
3. Goodstein, M., and Howe, A. "The Use of Concrete Methods in Secondary Chemistry Instruction." Journal of Research in Science Teaching, 15:361-366; September 1978.
4. Herron, D. "Role of Learning and Development: Critique of Novak's Comparison of Ausubel and Piaget." Science Education, 62:593-605; October-December 1978.
5. Karplus, R., Karplus, E., Formisano, M., and Paulsen, A. "A Survey of Proportional Reasoning and Control of Variables in Seven Countries." Journal of Research in Science Teaching, 14:411-471; September 1977.
6. Kolodiy, G. "Cognitive Development and Science Teaching." Journal of Research in Science Teaching, 14:21-26; January 1977.
7. Lawson, A., Karplus, R., and Adi, H. "The Acquisition of Propositional Logic and Formal Operational Schemata During the Secondary School Years." Journal of Research in Science Teaching, 15:465-478; November 1978.
8. Lawson, A., and Renner, J. "Relationships of Science Subject Matter and Developmental Levels of Learners." Journal of Research in Science Teaching, 12:347-358; October 1975.
9. Levine, D., and Linn, M. "Scientific Reasoning Ability in Adolescence: Theoretical Viewpoints and Educational Implications." Journal of Research in Science Teaching, 14:371-384; September 1977.
10. Lovell, K. "A Follow-up Study of Inhelder and Piaget's The Growth of Logical Thinking." British Journal of Psychology, 52:143-153; No. 2, 1961.
11. Padilla, M.J., Okey, J., and Dillashaw, F.G. "The Relationship between Science Process Skill and Formal Thinking Abilities." Paper presented at the National Association of Research in Science Teaching Annual Meeting, New York City, April 1981.
12. Piaget, J. Psychology of Intelligence. Littlefield, Adams and Co., Paterson, NJ, 1963.
13. Renner, J., Grant, R., and Sutherland, J. "Content and Concrete Thought." Science and Education, 62:215-221, April-June 1978.
14. Science 5/13. Macdonald Educational, London, England, 1972.
15. Science Curriculum Improvement Study. Rand McNally, Chicago, IL, 1970-74.

Developmental Characteristics in the Concrete Operational Stage

- Can solve logical problems through manipulation of concrete objects or experience only
- Can mentally reverse actions and operations
- Can classify and order objects
- Can understand that objects do not change in volume, weight, or number when they are spatially rearranged (conservation)
- Cannot identify and control variables, use proportional reasoning or propositional logic or generate multiple possibilities
- Cannot reason in the abstract

Developmental Characteristics in the Formal Operational Stage

- Can interact in the hypothetical
- Can formulate and test hypotheses by identifying and controlling variables
- Can generate multiple possibilities
- Can reflect on his/her own thought processes
- Can solve problems using proportional thought processes

Designing Science Lessons to Promote Cognitive Growth

Harvey Williams
C. William Turner
Lucien Debreuil
John Fast
John Berestiansky

Jean Piaget's view that a child's degree of intellectual development results from both *maturation* of the nervous system and *experience* has helped science educators to understand why John or Susan may not yet be able to learn specific science concepts. It has been less helpful in showing us what, if anything, we can do to encourage cognitive growth—largely because Piaget's analysis of logic is so complex.

What we hope to do here is to restate Piaget's model so that it relates directly to teaching and learning science. In doing so, we will describe intellectual activities that are readily observed in the science classroom (we call them "logical actions") and show how specific science lessons for junior high and secondary students can be designed to encourage cognitive development.

Our description grows out of work we have conducted cooperatively over the past six years. We welcome reader comments and suggestions that may help us further refine our endeavor.

Before describing our work, we feel it appropriate to make a few points about the nature of models. Behaviorist theory, which has dominated much of the research on knowledge and learning in the twentieth century, has focused on relationships between stimuli and responses, avoiding consideration of factors that might intervene between the two. [3]

Because the inadequacy of this approach has become more and more evident, psychologists have recently increased their efforts to formulate *models of mental processes* that might intervene between stimuli and responses. That is, just as physical scientists formulate models that make observable phenomena more predictable, psychologists have formulated models that may render human behavior more predictable.

Piaget's theory of cognitive development, to consider the case in point, is a model of the intellectual structures that develop from infancy to adulthood. But it can no more be taken as an absolute description of intellectual development than can a physical scientist's description of the atom in terms of quantum mechanics.

TWO KINDS OF KNOWLEDGE

Piaget distinguishes between two kinds of knowledge: *figurative* and *operative*. [2] Figurative knowledge relates to *factual* material, such as names of parts of speech, multiplication tables, and dates and descriptions of events. Operative knowledge consists of the ability to *apply logical processes* to what has been learned figuratively. [1]

Obviously these two forms of knowledge are interdependent. For instance, in order for a child to perform certain kinds of logical operations with numbers, he or she must have memorized the multiplication tables. On the other hand, some kinds of mathematical operations may be performed without knowledge that the multiplication tables even exist.

The ability to learn figuratively seems to be present early in infancy. The development of operative capability (or cognitive development) appears to progress through a series of stages, increasing roughly with age up to a level that varies from person to person and is not completed until late adolescence, if at all. In his model of cognitive development, Piaget identifies four such stages: the pre-verbal *sensori-motor* stage, the *pre-operational* stage (dominated by perception); the *concrete operational* stage (in which the youngster can solve problems related only to concrete objects); and finally—the *formal operational* stage, which at least some youngsters begin to reach at ages 11 and 12, and which is marked by the ability to handle abstractions and hypotheses.

Cognitive development appears to result from a combination of the child's biological development and his or her efforts to make sense out of experience. While the school can do little about biological development, it can stimulate cognitive development by providing opportunities for operative as well as figurative learning.

Although it is not known what constitutes an optimum mix of operative and figurative learning, we believe that there may be an overemphasis on figurative learning, both in schools generally and in science in particular. It may be that teachers are not sufficiently aware of the distinction between the two kinds of learning. Or it may be that figurative learning often masquerades as operative learning—especially when the learners' verbal explanations of concepts deceive the teacher into believing operative learning has occurred. The teacher faced with 30 or more students per class does not have time to probe beneath the verbal explanations. But he or she should keep in mind that operative learning occurs only when a youngster has solved a problem or found an answer using his or her own reasoning powers.

PERCEPTION AND LOGIC

A second important distinction made by Piaget is between *perception* and *logical operation*. At an early stage of development, a child tends to respond to things perceived, to that which is immediate and attention-grabbing. Piaget uses the term "perception-bound" to describe this kind of response. Later, the child begins to operate logically on his perceptions.

To some degree, we all tend to be perception-bound unless we stop to reflect on what we perceive. One good example occurred recently in a seventh-grade classroom, where the students were shown a 1000-ml graduated cylinder and a 500-ml beaker, and asked how many beakers of water would be required to fill the graduate. Most of the class responded on a perceptual basis at first, focusing on the relative *heights* of the two containers. Though they knew the volumes of the two vessels, they suggested that it would take four or five beakers of water to fill the graduate. Once the students paused to reflect, however, most were able to predict correctly that two beakers of water would fill the graduate.

Closely related to the concept of perception-bound is that of "centering." A learner may center on a single facet of a situation and be unable to expand the scope of his perception or logical activity to encompass other aspects of the situation. In the case of the beaker and graduated cylinder, learners centered on the relative heights of the two containers and had to "decenter" in order to take into account the greater diameter of the beaker.

Logical errors may be committed by both children and adults when faced with problems containing unfamiliar elements, too many elements, or elements that run counter to their past experience. Under these conditions, the learner is likely to center on those elements of the problem that attract his attention, though these may *not* be essential to solving the problem.

An example of centering was observed recently in an eighth-grade science classroom, where the students were doing a worksheet in which calories were computed from a given mass of water and temperature change. One child had worked the problems on the first half of the sheet correctly by multiplying grams of water times °C temperature change. However on the second half of the page, he reversed the operation and was dividing the water mass by the temperature change. When asked why he was dividing instead of multiplying, he pointed out that in these problems, the temperature had gone down instead of up. Therefore, it seemed proper to him to divide instead of multiply. This student had centered on the relationship between the arithmetical operation and the change in temperature. The number of elements involved in the concept of "calories" (in the quantitative sense) was apparently too great for him to manage.

Discovering that the length of a pendulum determines the period of its swing is a popular activity in process-oriented classrooms, where it is used to illustrate scientific method. By experimenting with the pendulum, the student is supposed to learn to identify and control variables. But studies suggest that few junior high students understand the logic of the experiment even after they have performed it and arrived at the proper conclusion. We have had students state the principle of the pendulum correctly, then attempt to "prove" it by demonstration. In the end, they convinced themselves that the mass of the bob determines the pendulum's period.

The number of variables in the experiment; the dependent variable (swings per minute or frequency, however it is stated); and the relationships between these factors constitute an overwhelming number of elements to be encompassed by the developing cognitive structures of many adolescents. The child centers on only one or two of the possible independent variables (usually mass of the bob and length of the pendulum or amplitude of the swing), but is unable to think of others at the same time or to separate and control these variables successfully. Even students who have just studied the pendulum and passed a teacher's written test (figurative learning) are likely to become confused when asked to perform the experiment independently. We would wager that, a few weeks later, very few eighth-grade students would be able to explain the activity successfully.

Piaget's analysis of the reasoning process is based on a form of symbolic logic and Boolean algebra. What follows is our attempt to present his analysis in terms of intellectual activities more readily observed in science learning situations. As mentioned previously, we have applied the term "logical actions" to these intellectual activities, and they have been illustrated by commonly taught concepts and activities. The Piagetian stage of logical operation attributable to such action follows in parentheses.

LOGICAL ACTIONS
Actions Involved in Classifying

1. Simple classifying—Items can be grouped according to a single attribute *(concrete)*. Example: Rocks can be classified according to texture (fine and coarse).

2. Complex classifying—Items can be grouped according to two or more attributes at the same time *(concrete-formal)*. Example: In addition to texture, rocks can be grouped into dark and light so that four groups result (fine-dark, coarse-dark, fine-light, and coarse-light).

3. Hierarchical classifying—Items can be grouped according to a single attribute, after which the resulting groups can be further subdivided by another attribute *(concrete-formal)*. Example: Mammals can be subdivided into dogs and mammals other than dogs; dogs can be further subdivided into poodles and dogs other than poodles; etc. Similarly, mammals other than dogs can be subdivided.

Actions Involved in Seriating

1. Simple seriating—A single relationship between items can be ordered *(concrete)*. Example: Items can be arranged according to size so that the smallest is first and the largest last.

2. Complex seriating—A number of relationships between items can be ordered *(concrete-formal)*. Example: Items which have been arranged according to size can also be arranged by mass, so that the lightest is first and heaviest last. A figure such as the following would result:

The concept of density is often taught this way. Density also involves proportional reasoning.

Actions Involved in Inductive Reasonings

Making generalizations based on a number of individual observations:

a. Nonquantitative *(concrete)*. Example: Discovering momentum by noting that moving objects displace stationary objects when they collide. It may even be noted that the amount of displacement is related to the mass and/or velocity of the moving object and inversely related to the mass of the stationary object.

b. Quantitative *(formal)*. Example: Quantifying and generalizing results of the experiment described under *a*.

Actions Involved in Probabilistic Thinking

Inferring from observations that are somewhat inconsistent by considering the relative frequency of events or objects *(formal)*. Examples: 1) Rain is usually associated with clouds, though the presence of clouds does not necessarily mean rain. Still, the probability of rain is higher when there are clouds. 2) The concept of experimental errors.

Actions Involved in Logical Deduction

1. Formulating hypotheses (logical inference)—Using logic to deduce or infer the consequences of a set of conditions *(formal)*. Example: Conditions—Force accelerates objects, the amount of acceleration being inversely proportional to the mass of the object but directly proportional to the magnitude of the force. Earth's gravity determines a force that is directly proportional to the mass of the object upon which it acts. Hypothesis: Heavy objects (more massive) and light objects (less massive) will fall with a common acceleration; that is, will experience the same set of speeds.

2. Testing Hypotheses—Considering all possible factors related to a hypothesized event or relationship and:

a. Identifying relevant variables,

b. Controlling variables in all possible combinations (combinatorial thinking) so as to test them out one at a time,

c. Eliminating contradictions by recognizing and eliminating variables that result in contradictions *(formal)*. Example: The pendulum experiment described previously. All possible independent variables must be considered, including: length, mass of bob, amplitude of swing, impetus or push. Each must be tested for at least two values while all others are held constant and their effect on the dependent variable (frequency) observed.

Actions Involved in Proportional Reasoning

Compensating for change in one variable by changing another in the same proportion so that a system remains constant *(formal)*. Example: Boyle's Law, which explains the relationship between pressure and volume of gases; an increase in pressure is compensated by a decrease in volume so that the product *(P X V)* remains constant.

PLANNING FOR OPERATIVE LEARNING

In planning operative learning experiences, the teacher must first consider the level of cognitive development of the learner. *Most children in junior high school will be in a transitional stage between concrete and formal operations.* Thus, time spent having junior high school students perform and write up experiments in a manner that includes a hypothesis and the other trappings of scientific research may be time wasted because most junior high students are not at the formal operational level.

Operative learning occurs only when a student solves a problem or finds an answer by his or her own reasoning. If the teacher has dictated the conclusion which is recorded in notebooks at the end of an experiment, the students have not engaged in operative learning. (Students might benefit more from the old method of stating a principle and performing an experiment to illustrate the principle. At least they would then have some idea what was going on.)

As good teachers have recognized for a long time, operative learning may be provided for through such diverse means as class discussion, demonstrations, laboratory activities, media, written assignments, reading assignments, and field trips. What is required is an interesting situation in which the teacher poses a problem or asks a question that challenges the learners to arrive at a solution or answer that makes sense to them.

The difficulty of planning for operative learning should not be underestimated. Operative learning experiences tend to be less satisfying to students conditioned in the figurative learning tradition. And planning operative learning experiences requires that the teacher be familiar with Piaget's model of the structure of logical thought as well as being well-grounded in science. Students in the same class may be at different levels of cognitive development. We have found students who appeared to be functioning at an almost preoperational level in classrooms with students who were functioning at the level of formal operations. Finally, an operative learning experience is possible only if the learner is *actively engaged* in thinking, making motivation an important factor.

ACTIVITY WITH "SHIFTING SAND"

Over the past few years, we have been devising science learning activities designed specifically to provide operative learning experiences. In so doing, we have tried to incorporate the logical actions (classifying, seriating, and so forth) identified earlier. We have also tried to incorporate other insights from Piaget's model—that is, we hope to encourage operative learning by giving students needed opportunity to reflect and react logically rather than simply perceive, plus the opportunity to expand the scope of their perception or logical activity. We also try to devise highly motivating experiences that will actively engage students in learning.

One example is provided by an activity called "A Close Look at Sand Grains."

In the activity, students examine sand with a hand lens and describe the shapes, colors, sizes, and other characteristics they see. They then divide approximately 50 of the grains into two groups on the basis of any characteristic they choose, and try to subdivide this grouping. Later they are asked to divide the grains into dark and light, to calculate the percent of each category, and to observe the reaction between hydrochloric acid and both limestone and sand.

In the teacher's guide (see Figure 1) five elements to the activity are outlined: (1) logical actions, (2) concepts and processes of science, (3) approach, (4) closure, and (5) materials. Note that the teacher's guide does suggest that effort should be focused on the sand grains' physical attributes and alerts teachers to the fact that pupils functioning at the concrete operational stage will be unable to reason in terms of percentages. (Obviously, students should not be penalized for having only progressed to a stage of intellectual maturity which is characteristic of their age.)

We hope that the difficulties facing a teacher who would plan operative learning experiences will not prove discouraging, though we do wish to underscore the complexity of the problem and the degree of commitment required. Piaget has provided educators with valuable insight into the nature of learning—it is up to us to explore this insight fully and capitalize on it to help students learn science.

REFERENCES
1. Elkind, David. *Child Development and Education.* Oxford University Press, New York, N.Y. 1976.
2. Lawson, Anton E., J. D. Blake, and Floyd H. Nordlund. "Training Effects and Generalization of the Ability to Control Variables in High School Biology Students." *Science Education* 59(3):387-396.
3. Piaget, Jean. *Science Education and the Psychology of the Child.* The Viking Press, New York, N.Y. 1972.
4. Sprinthall, R. C. and N. A. Sprinthall. *Educational Psychology: A Developmental Approach.* Addison-Wesley Publishing Co., Menlo Park, Calif. 1974.
5. Wollman, Warren. "Intellectual Development Beyond Elementary School VI. Controlling Variables: Survey." Lawrence Hall of Science, University of California, Berkeley, Calif. 1976. ED 132 055.

Figure 1
A Close Look at Sand Grains—Teacher's Guide

1. **Logical actions.** Simple classifying, proportional thinking, probabilistic thinking.
2. **Concepts and Processes of Science.**
   Concepts:
   Sedimentary rock is formed from materials that have settled to the bottom of the sea. Sandstone is formed from sand particles.
   Sand particles are often made up of different minerals.
   Processes: Classifying, using numbers, inferring, measuring.
3. **Approach.** The activity should be undertaken with a minimum of teacher guidance. Pupils should be encouraged to make accurate representations of the sand grains. The most difficult problem will be the calculations and interpretations of percents.
4. **Closure.** Effort should be focused on the attributes of sand grains. The most difficult task will be assisting in the interpretation of percentage. Pupils functioning at the concrete operational stage will be unable to reason in terms of percentages.
5. **Materials.** Sand, the more heterogeneous, the better. A pinch per pupil, hand lenses, or dissecting microscopes.

Reasoning About Spatial Relationships

Michael J. Wavering
Linda J. Kelsey

Do your students still have trouble with maps, seasons, visualizing blueprints or clothing patterns, origami, or coordinate systems such as longitude and latitude? All these topics require reasoning about objects in space.

Recent research findings often characterize middle school students as "transitional." In a Piagetian sense, their reasoning patterns are assumed to be sometimes upper level concrete and at other times formal in nature. However, such assumptions may not be valid for spatial reasoning. Research into specific areas of spatial relationships shows that many middle school students have difficulty with even the lower level concrete structures. Middle school students show a particularly wide range of individual spatial reasoning abilities, consistent with their varied abilities in other areas.

Piaget and Inhelder* assert that reasoning about space requires more than just perception. What students "see" is usually determined by the mental structures they have, and not conversely. Three areas of spatial reasoning have been delineated. Topological space deals with nearness, separation, order, continuity and boundaries of objects or groups of objects. Most middle school learners have developed the structures of topological space, but some may still have trouble with a continuous figure being made up of a series of points (for example, points along a line).

Projective space involves "points of view" and the ability to coordinate different perspectives using above-below, left-right and before-behind relationships. Middle school students may have trouble visualizing how a set of objects would appear from the side (as in a mechanical drawing class) or how lunar phases, seasons, or eclipses occur. Projective space is also concerned with the idea of perspective where parallel lines appear to converge in the distance, causing student difficulties in making and interpreting perspective drawings.

Euclidean space deals with reference frames, coordinate systems and plane geometry. Lengths, areas and volumes are constant regardless of point of view. These notions are difficult for most middle school students. They may be unable to locate objects in two or three dimensions, such as in graphing data or using maps or coordinate systems. Reasoning about horizontals or verticals may also be difficult, and water levels in containers may be depicted as remaining parallel to the container rather than horizontal when the container is tilted.

Much of the content taught in science courses requires spatial reasoning, especially when presented in traditional formats. Textbook and blackboard drawings, slides and movies all use a two-dimensional format to present three-dimensional

---

*Piaget, Jean and Barbel Inhelder. *The Child's Conceptions of Space*. W.W. Norton and Company, Inc. New York, 1967.

Art by Lydia Nolan-Davis

systems. Students who don't have well-developed projective reasoning abilities cannot understand the concepts being presented. Locating points on a map or graph requires the realization that two separate coordinates are needed instead of just distances. Interpreting three-dimensional coordinate systems (such as elevation lines on maps or depth in a perspective drawing) is nearly impossible for most middle school students. If traditional formats fail to gain student understanding of these science concepts, are there alternatives?

Piaget and Inhelder repeatedly emphasize that concrete level students must manipulate objects to develop spatial reasoning structures. The first step in the classroom should be to provide activities where students can interact on an individual basis with objects. Students create their own mental structures by mentally organizing their actions. Demonstrations and lectures by the teacher are not a substitute. Activities should be designed to require the student to find the solution to a problem using the objects provided. For example, students may be asked to devise a model to explain phases of the moon using styrofoam balls and a light source, or to make a model of the classroom and predict what it would look like from different points of view. The science classroom provides a unique setting for manipulating simple equipment to provide opportunities to help develop reasoning abilities, especially in the spatial area. In addition, middle school students are particularly receptive to teaching strategies in which they are actively involved.

It is important that middle school level students experience a wide variety of activities. We may have to sacrifice "covering" large amounts of content in order to provide time for activities that involve concrete level spatial structures which are an essential part of intellectual development and are necessary prerequisites for formal thought.

Your Child:
Middle/Junior High School Years

New York State United Teachers

One day she spells her name "Sherri" and walks into class wearing high heels and a thick layer of makeup. The next day she is back to being the thumb-sucking "Sherry" who wants to listen to a tape of "Rumpelstiltskin." She is a seventh grader and for her and her peers the Middle School years are indeed the best of times and the worst of times. She is continually asking herself—and others—Who am I? How do I fit into the scheme of things?

MANY CHANGES

As Middle School students, Sherry and her peers have moved from the security of a self-contained elementary classroom, the comfort of being a closely knit, compact group of 20 to 30 kids for whom one teacher supplies all needs, to the complexity of a school day divided by 7 different classes in which they must learn to get along with upwards of 1,000 students. Suddenly they must learn to work with many different teachers and to share those teachers with hundreds of other students. They move from an integrated day to one that changes continuously. Just as they get used to one class, the bell rings and they must move on to a different class.

Middle School students aren't just changing classes; they are changing in their physical and emotional needs. Many demands are placed on them: they are expected to "grow up," assume responsibility, become independent, make decisions. At the same time, they are discovering their own sexuality and being challenged by drugs and other shifting social codes. They feel inadequate; they want to be popular but aren't sure how to go about it. Middle School students are continually doing things to make adults—and other students—notice them: they giggle a lot, run in the halls, punch each other, wear funny clothes (Don't think your child is the only one wearing 3 pairs of socks!). They laugh a lot; they cry a lot. The lives of Middle School students are punctuated by times of great highs and great lows; enthusiasm changes to despair in a flash. As one Middle School teacher put it, "Parents and teachers of Middle School students need patience, positive reinforcement, and a good handkerchief."

MAKING THE MOST OF NEW OPPORTUNITIES

Parents should be aware of the opportunities the Middle School offers for discovering what their child does best. For those who excel academically, accelerated courses are available. Clubs and special activities offer the chance for enrichment. All students can take many classes in which they have a new opportunity to shine: industrial arts, home economics, visual and performing arts. Parents should be aware of the opportunity of discovering extra-academic abilities in their children. Parents should find what their children do best and build on that. For example, success in cross-country running can lead the way to a new-found success in reading. Once a Middle School child discovers he can succeed in one thing, he is more likely to believe he can overcome failure in something else.

HELPING YOUR CHILD AT HOME

Parents can play a crucial role in their child's Middle School years in other ways. There are some specific things they can do:

- Parents can put themselves at the child's disposal at a set time every day, even if it is just for 15 minutes. This can be a time to help with homework, help with social entanglements—or just to listen.
- Parents can turn off the TV for a certain period every evening. It is hard for Johnny to study if everyone else gets to watch TV. Moreover, Johnny is not likely to read if Mom and Dad don't read.
- Parents can institute a "sharing time" with their Middle School students:
  — Ask the child his opinion of an event in the newspaper;
  — Ask the child to explain the metric system;
  — Share a joke: you read me an elephant joke and I'll tell you a joke I liked as a kid;
  — Share an amusing poem (anthologies by David McCord, John Ciardi, Shel Silverstein, William Cole, Nikke Giovanni are recommended). One Middle School teacher gave poems as homework, with the instruction: "Your parent must sign that you read this poem aloud." Parents wrote back, "Please send more. We had a hilarious time."
- Think of ways the student can practice his skills:
  — If the family is planning a trip, ask the child to chart it on the map (he's learning map skills in social studies);
  — Ask the child to make out the grocery list, finding "best buys" in the newspaper;
  — Encourage the child to write notes to family and friends in other towns;
  — If you order from a catalogue, ask the child to make out the order blank.

These types of activities are interesting and even enjoyable ways for parents to share time with their children and to help children see the practical importance of what they are learning in school. The Middle Schooler is developing a social and ethical sense: he is interested in justice, in right and wrong, in politics. Encourage him to write Letters to the Editor, letters to his Congressmen. One nice thing—they usually answer.

WORKING TOGETHER

If your child frequently tells you he has no homework, phone the school. Middle School students usually have a tremendous amount of homework, and most teachers place considerable importance on its completion. Your child will benefit most from the education he receives during these critical years if you play an active role. Children need the support of both teachers and parents. Get to know each of your child's teachers. They are trained professionals, and realize the importance of your active participation.

Teaching Strategies

Becoming a teacher is largely a do-it-yourself job.

Walter Farmer and Margaret Farrell
*Systematic Instruction in Science
for the Middle and High School Years*

Knowledge acquisition for this age group (early adolescents) will involve helping students to gain information through the printed word, through direct observation of objects and events, and through use of community resources. Teachers need to learn how to facilitate knowledge acquisition in ways that are meaningful to a diverse population of students.

Paul DeHart Hurd, et al.
*The Status of Middle School and
Junior High School Science*

The best hope for the teacher is to do for her students what she likes done for herself in university classes: to be intellectually engaged, challenged, and excited, as much as the infant is when he explores a wooden block or a toy, or as a scientist is when he studies the atom.

Milton Schwebel and Jane Raph
Piaget in the Classroom

Classroom Management

Johanna Strange
Stephen A. Henderson

For two decades science educators have encouraged teachers to use activity-based science instruction in their classrooms. Even at the elementary level, science instruction is considered ineffective unless students are investigating with hands-on materials.

So why are some teachers still reluctant to implement activity-based science programs? The biggest stumbling block to the success of laboratory science has been teachers' fear of working in unstructured, disorganized, undisciplined, noisy, chaotic classrooms. Hands-on science may, at times, appear unstructured, noisy, and even chaotic, but it is well-designed chaos. Organization and classroom management are the keys to success.

Where can we acquire the necessary management skills? How do we create a classroom that is attractive and stimulating? What procedures aid in the management of an activity-based science program? The model presented here combines a less restricted environment, with enough organization and structure to maintain order during activity-based instruction.

THE CLASSROOM

Psychologist Robert Gagne emphasizes that "the essential task of the teacher is to arrange conditions of the learner's environment so that processes of learning will be activated, supported, enhanced, and maintained." (3)* In the classroom, this means providing a bright, well-decorated environment, enhanced by interests centers, bulletin boards, posters, and other visual displays.

Students need opportunities to interact, share ideas, and draw upon each other's discoveries. The physical arrangement of the classroom must encourage student interaction. Straight rows of desks all facing the same direction, for example, impede the development of strong, activity-oriented science programs.

Although extremely important, the physical setting is actually secondary to classroom management, the heart and soul of effective instruction. The management procedure described here includes five phases: teacher/student preparation, pre-activity discussion, distribution of materials, experimentation, and discussion and clean-up.

PHASE 1: TEACHER-STUDENT PREPARATION

To begin, define your instructional objective and select an appropriate activity. Scrutinize the activity you have in mind for pitfalls and problems; then collect the materials you will need. Give thought to the room arrangement and logistics required for the activity.

---

*See References.

Once you have decided on an activity, divide the class into teams. Teams of two to four seem to promote good verbal interaction and involvement in classroom investigations. Even if the explorations are pursued individually, students need a group with which to identify. Try to divide students equally by sex and seat team members close together.

Assign each person in the group a number and give each group a name: Newton's Team, Einstein's team, or a title of the group members' choice. Naming the teams encourages participation in group investigations and aids the smooth distribution and collection of equipment.

Before the activity, organize materials at four stations around the room. Team members should share responsibility for gathering and returning materials, thus eliminating confusion and expediting delivery of materials.

PHASE 2: PRE-ACTIVITY DISCUSSION

During the second phase, students identify the problem, design an experiment, determine data-collecting and record-keeping procedures, and decide what equipment they need. Discussing the activity, explaining procedures, exchanging experiences, and even arguing with each other promotes learning during this phase. This allows students time to develop their ideas and form associations.

Effective questioning plays a vital role. Design questions that are open-ended to stimulate a creative exchange of ideas, yet directed toward goals such as experimental design or data collection. It is most important to establish a reason for doing the activity. As students agree on investigating procedures, list the necessary equipment on the blackboard. This equipment should already be assembled at the collection stations.

PHASE 3: DISTRIBUTION OF EQUIPMENT

Assign students collection tasks by numbers such as: ones collect paper towels and vials, twos collect plants, and so on. If the activity requires more than one piece of equipment, note the quantity on the board. Students should not begin to collect equipment until all have received their assignments. Set a time limit for gathering materials. After the equipment is collected, check to be certain each team has all necessary supplies.

PHASE 4: EXPERIMENTATION

With all teams and equipment in place, experimenting can begin. Review the process with the students. If the team is to work as a group, assign tasks by numbers to ensure group involvement. Stress the importance of thorough observation and record-keeping. All observations should be noted on the record sheet designed earlier. Your behavior is very important. Move about the classroom, asking questions, stimulating thought, and keeping students on task.

During these phases, teachers often worry about the noise level. Teachers should expect and encourage communication among students in activity-oriented programs. Stand back; listen to the activity in your classroom. Rank the noise level on a scale of one to ten: one for silence, ten for bedlam, and identify the expected noise level range. Praise students who cooperate rather than criticize those who do not. If certain children cause problems, remove them from the activity and let them watch. They'll soon want to participate.

PHASE 5: DISCUSSION AND CLEAN-UP

The final phase incorporates review, compilation of the students' data, and discussion. Data can be graphed, discrepancies discussed, and consensus reached. Be sure conclusions are understood by all. Afterward, students clean, disassemble, and return the equipment to its original locations. Allow time for thorough clean-up; it's best not to excuse any student until all complete their clean-up tasks.

THE TEACHER

While organization is critical to activity-based instruction, success also depends upon the teacher. Enthusiastic, flexible, energetic, humanistic teachers best suit the methods described here. Teachers also contribute to the students' willingness to learn and sense of security by showing respect, speaking politely, and listening unhurriedly to each child.

These are important traits in any teaching situation, but they are vital to success in hands-on activities. Science programs flounder when students grow passive or bored. Effective activity-based programs combine stimulating environment with skillful management to make children active learners.

REFERENCES
1. Abruscato, Joe, and Jack Hassard. *Loving and Beyond: Science Teaching for the Humanistic Classroom.* Goodyear Publishing Company, Inc., Pacific Palisades, CA. 1976.
2. Dyrli, Odvard E. "Should We Scrap Lab-Centered Science Programs?" *Learning*, 9:34-39; February 1981.
3. Hart, Leslie A. "Don't Teach Them; Help Them Learn." *Learning* 9:38-40; March 1981.
4. Martin, Robert J. *Teaching Through Encouragement.* Prentice-Hall, Inc., Englewood Cliffs, NJ. 1980.

Leadership Strategies in the Middle School Science Classroom

Carlton W. Knight II
Gary E. Dunkleberger

Worrying about student behavior can have an inhibiting effect upon the quality of science taught in middle school and junior high classrooms. Although a high level of verbal and physical interaction is usually desirable, teachers are often reluctant to conduct student-centered science activities for fear of being unable to control disruptive pupil behavior. Whether faced with excessive enthusiasm generated by dramatic demonstrations or the malicious destruction of equipment, teachers may feel ill-prepared to handle these behavior patterns, and the science lab will not be presented. Thus, both students and teachers are deprived of worthwhile activity-oriented experiences.

Effective student control, where students have the freedom to interact and yet are under the guidance of the teacher, is not the result of using any specific procedure or technique. Positive control comes from the successful interaction of many components, including personalities, nonverbal communications, attitudes, classroom rules, weather, dress, room color and arrangement, activity procedures, and leadership strategies.

The leadership strategies required to establish and maintain the desired student behavioral standards should be given major consideration. You as the teacher are the leader of your classroom. Because of your position, students usually challenge you to define the strength and parameters of your leadership. Students try to determine whether you mean what you say. Does "quiet" really mean quiet, or does it mean "lower your voice"? Does "please get to work" mean get to work, or "sit quietly and don't bother me"? When homework assignments given Monday are due on Tuesday, does it mean Tuesday, or is Wednesday also acceptable? The effectiveness of many science activities depends ultimately upon your ability to maintain the desired behavioral standards in class.

The relationship between teachers and their classes often begins with a period of peaceful coexistence, when teachers and students react friendly, but passively, while each seeks more information about the other. This stage of goodwill may mislead a teacher into a false sense of security. Initial challenges to the teacher's leadership are usually subtle, seemingly inconsequential, often overlooked. By assuming a firm relationship has been established and not reacting to initial challenges, teachers allow gradual undermining of their authority.

If each day your science class takes longer to begin, lab materials are stored less orderly, and homework assignments are turned in at increasingly later dates, it is time for you to reflect on how you could have prevented these behavior patterns from developing. Some teachers might be reluctant to counteract these minor infractions because the class relationship is seemingly off to a positive start. But initial incidents can progress in frequency and seriousness until teachers lose effective control of the classroom. Science lessons and labs are conducted and students learn, but not at the optimum level. Unfortunately, it is sometimes easier to lower standards rather than expend energy to maintain them.

Art by Lydia Nolan-Davis

TEACHER STRATEGIES

Here is one strategy designed to help you gain positive pupil behavior by using initial student challenges to your advantage. Rather than waiting until these incidents become major tests of power, be prepared to react to students' subtle first challenges.

In the science classroom where the rule, "When the bell rings, it is a signal for the teacher to stop, not for the students to leave" applies, the initial student challenge may occur during a busy lab when you are conferring with a team in the back of the room, unaware that the period has ended. The bell suddenly rings and, before you can finish your conversation and give cleanup directions, half the class leaves the room. Now you must salvage the remains of an unfortunate situation. Although the students' intent was not malicious, your leadership was successfully challenged and has been weakened.

A more desirable circumstance is to plan the initial lab using minimal materials. Carefully monitor the clock so when the period ends you are near the door, conferring with a student team. As soon as some of the class tries to leave, you can easily block their exit and politely remind them of the rule. Because minimal equipment is used, there is sufficient time for students to clean up and be on time for the next period. A gentle reminder and strategic positioning turns a minor student challenge into a rule reinforcement experience. You control the challenge process in a positive, pre-planned way rather than hastily reacting to the unexpected.

Another example is the starting time of the science class. If a specified time or bell designates when socializing ceases and the class begins, an important issue is whether or not the class will respect the rule even if you are not present. If you intentionally wait outside the door talking to another student after the designated time, you can observe the class and if necessary politely remind the class of your rule. The alternative is to wait until a hall emergency demands your presence and hope the students will remain quiet during your absence.

The same strategy can be applied successfully to science homework. If the first few assignments are simple and require minimal time to complete, everyone can easily do them in a few minutes after school. Because excuses for not doing homework are less valid, you are in a position to encourage punctuality and responsibility. If the initial assignments are complicated and time consuming, it may be difficult to determine the validity of the excuses and your leadership credibility may suffer. By conditioning students to be on time at the beginning of the term, you increase the probability of the same behavior continuing once assignments become more difficult.

The preceding examples illustrate how being aware of subtle student challenges, and reacting to them, can help establish effective standards for student behavior. The point is to show that you expect specific rules or policies to be followed, not to entrap or intimidate students.

Effective control allows the talking, questioning, equipment handling, and moving inherent in early adolescents. It is the teacher's responsibility not only to teach the science curriculum, but to do so in an environment where pupil interaction enhances rather than limits learning opportunities.

BIBLIOGRAPHY

Dobson, J. *Dare to Discipline*. Tyndale House Publishers, Wheaton, Illinois. 1972.

Gray, J. *The Teacher's Survival Guide*. Lear Siegler, Inc./Fearon Publishers, Belmont, California. 1974.

Long, J.D., and V.H. Frye. *Making It Till Friday: A Guide to Successful Classroom Management*. Princeton Book Company, Princeton, New Jersey. 1977.

Macht, J. *Teacher Teachim: The Toughest Game in Town*. John Wiley & Sons, Inc., New York City. 1975.

Madsen, C. Jr., and C.W. Madsen. *Teaching-Discipline: A Positive Approach for Educational Development*. Allyn and Bacon, Boston, Massachusetts. 1974.

Martin, R., and D. Lauridsen. *Developing Student Discipline and Motivation: A Series for Teaching Inservice Training*. Research Press, Champaign, Illinois. 1974.

Sloane, H.N. *Classroom Management: Remediation and Prevention*. John Wiley & Sons, New York City. 1976.

Tanner, L. *Classroom Discipline for Effective Teaching and Learning*. Holt, Rinehart & Winston, New York City. 1978.

Responsibility: Discipline Inside-Out

Nancy Doda

PRINCIPLES OF RESPONSIBILITY-TAKING

Admit it! You have caught yourself daydreaming about students who are independent, dependable, responsible *or* fantasizing about teaching in a high school *or* wishing you could close your eyes, whisk a magic wand and have your kids suddenly transformed into responsible young adolescents. Don't feel badly, because you're not alone. Anyone who works with middle school kids shares the same plaguing preoccupation with responsible behavior, and how to get it. Parents echo teachers with their comments about their kids: "They won't do their homework unless I nag," "They are lazy," "They won't do their chores." What parents and teachers really want to know is how they can get youngsters to take responsibility without having to threaten, nag, or entice them.

Unfortunately, there are never easy answers to hard questions, but there are answers, nonetheless. Before tackling the question of how to promote responsible behavior, I'd like to set forth some assumptions about responsibility and its development:

1. Taking on responsibility is risky, so middle school youngsters will only attempt it when they feel in control, on top of things, and safe from guaranteed failure.
2. Responsible behavior is behavior that demonstrates concern for others. Middle schoolers will learn to be responsible in the context of a fellowship of caring relationships with teachers and peers, where interdependence is as important as independence;
3. Responsibility emerges from personal success in responsible roles. Middle school learners need opportunities to be successful and productive in authentic ways;
4. Responsibility is holding up your side of a commitment. Middle school kids need practice in making and being held accountable for their commitments.
5. Responsible individuals take initiative. They're independent, rather than dependent. Middle school kids need the time, opportunity and encouragement to take initiative; to go it alone!
6. Responsibility matures slowly and public schools are not necessarily designed to promote real responsibility taking, so teachers have to fight both nature and the system. Believe it or not, though, schools can become places where kids grow in responsibility.

GROUNDWORK: CHANGING THE BIG PICTURE

Overall school features play an important role in the teaching of responsibility. Some schools are organized in ways which promote responsible student behavior; others are not. If middle schools want to make a grassroots effort to promote responsible behavior in students, then three priorities deserve their attention.

First, middle school youngsters are perpetually uneasy about themselves, others and their surroundings. This uneasiness is problematic when it comes to helping them towards responsibility taking. To reduce early adolescent uneasiness, and to increase middle school students' sense of personal control, middle schools should be organized so that each student sees his school world as reachable and controllable. Large and anonymous school environments produce kids who often feel alienated, powerless and ineffective, who shun responsibility and choose apathy and deviance instead. Smaller, more personal communities make it possible for students to be known and acknowledged as unique persons and meaningful contributers. Interdisciplinary teams or communities have provided large middle schools with one extremely viable organizational alternative.

Second, significant opportunities for decision-making responsibilities should not be limited to an elected student council designed to represent the whole school. Smaller communities must be accompanied by smaller more relevant governing arrangements, so that youngsters in middle schools do, in fact, contribute to the shape of their immediate school world. Student governing opportunities should be year-long components of instruction provided by the learning community. As an example, community decisions could be fed through community meetings run not only by teachers but by students as well. Students should be able to see the results of their personal contributions to the school community. They should be close enough to participate and to appreciate the products of their participation.

Third, middle schools need to make a once and for all commitment to involving the community in the teaching responsibility. Whether it takes place inside or outside school walls, youngsters must have opportunities to connect what they do in school with what's important in the larger society. Kids who spend afternoon upon afternoon watching TV, only participating vicariously in responsible social roles, desperately need authentic responsibility-taking experiences. The school could solicit help from individual community members and/or parents to provide apprenticeship experiences for its children. By cooperating with parents and community, such experiences could enrich curriculum, boost community-school relations and yield more responsible young adults.

These three priorities represent new horizons for middle schools. As we consider future organizational changes, we should examine ways in which our middle schools could be smaller, more personal communities, settings for participatory democracy and doors to the real live community.

BRINGING OUT THE BEST IN KIDS: TIPS FOR TEACHING RESPONSIBILITY
Rules: Reasons for Responsibility

Every classroom has procedures and expectations which provide structure for the learning situation. Often teachers generate reasonable and logical classroom rules, present them to students, and then are disappointed when kids ignore the rules. For middle school kids, simply obeying the *teacher's* rules yields very little personal satisfaction. Kids will only see rules as reasons for responsibility when they have had a chance to design the rules. Then, following the rules involves sticking to their word and not someone else's.

In addition to involving students in the creation of classroom rules, insist that every rule be understood in terms of the consequences it was designed to prevent. When the final list of rules is thoroughly discussed, refined and understood, post it as "We Agree" statements.

Even with well-developed rules, violations are inevitable. There are, however, several recommended measures teachers can take to further stimulate responsibility-taking when such violations do occur:

1. Curb your temptation to demand "Quiet" when noise is the disrupting behavior. While such demands and related threats may produce immediate results and may be at times almost necessary, they do not encourage responsible thinking and behavior. When possible, teachers should try to use any rule-violation as an opportunity to refer to the "We Agree" statements and their underlying reasons. Simply reminding students that they've made a deal and that they're responsible is far better than assuming the responsibility for controlling the change yourself.

2. You shouldn't be the only one in the classroom who's on the lookout for rule violation. Every student should have a rule buddy or coworker to assist him in following classroom rules. Students can often prevent problems from growing worse and they can help in making a classroom run more smoothly. Teachers can empower this rule buddy role by making reference to the rule buddy when a partner is at fault. Holding kids accountable for one another is a new concept for so many, so go slow at first!

3. Teachers that work together on teams should try to coordinate classroom rules so that students on a team can expect the same structure from class to class. This can work wonders with responsibility if the students are in on the rule writing.

What To Say, When and How?

Classrooms are filled with conversation. Teachers are continually talking to students, with students and sometimes even for students. Naturally, with so much instructional time devoted to talk, what we say, when and how, really makes a difference!

If we're concerned with developing more responsible students, we ought to be as careful with our use of praise as with our use of demands and threats. Praise may sound much nicer but it's not necessarily any better. In fact, research suggests that the extensive use of praise may promote student dependence, rather than independence. Students tend to learn very little about personal satisfaction and intrinsic rewards when they rely on teacher praise for guidance and support. As an alternative, teachers should work to initiate student self-appraisal, sharing in the pleasure that students find in their own successes.

In leading class discussions, conducting group lessons or just managing classroom affairs, teachers are more likely to encourage responsible behavior if they talk less, have students talk more and use student ideas in structuring the dialogue or discussion. Similarly, teachers who wait longer for a student response after asking a

PROJECT: DISCOVERY
1. Each group will cho...
2. Organization will b... the group's discretion.
3. Decide on appropr... ...uals
4. All group members ...e one area which to report.
5. Visual aids are enc...
6. D... ...n a deadli... ...within...

Art by Lydia Nolan-Davis

question encourage students to assume some responsibility for thinking of an answer. If the teacher asks a question, pauses, and then almost immediately calls on someone else or answers the question for the student, students will learn to sit back, relax and wait for someone else to get the job done.

There are other kinds of daily verbal interactions which can carry the responsibility message to students. In particular, teachers have to model independence and responsibility and can do so in a few simple ways. When you are really angered by students or other everyday happenings, try to take responsibility for your feelings. Try using what Gordon calls an "I Message" (*Teacher Effectiveness Training*, 1974). State how you're feeling, what's making you feel that way and what problem is caused for you by what's happening. Here's one:

"Tim, I get very frustrated when you keep tapping on your desk, because I can't concentrate while teaching this reading lesson." The responsible expression of feelings conveys an important message: I am feeling badly because of what you're doing and not because of who you are. Students won't feel crushed but will feel stimulated to respond, by changing what they're doing. That's a step toward responsibility.

Responsibility in Learning

Students vary in their ability to work successfully on independent learning tasks. To some, freedom is enticing; to others, it is intimidating. As a result, standard prescriptions for independent learning are rarely appropriate. Teachers need an array of options from which to choose. Here's a modest list of approaches that encourage responsibility:

1. During the course of a school year, give every child at least some chance to learn something on his own and in his own way. It may be that you select some small objective which the child learns using his own choice of resources in his personally created learning activities. Be sure that there is flexible classroom time so that students can, in fact, try out independent learning.
2. Have students work in learning teams with common learning goals. The team should be responsible for its members so that everyone must be sure that everyone else understands the assignment, completes the assignment and succeeds on the test. Evaluate the team's success.
3. Peer-teaching is an extremely useful way to encourage responsibility in modestly independent learners. Students can rely on their areas of expertise, can prepare for the actual teaching and can feel rewarded by the real responsibility inherent in someone else's learning.
4. Have students keep records of completed work so that they learn how to monitor their own progress. Make a checklist for each week or term and hold students accountable for accurate record keeping. Send a copy to the parents so that responsibility is reinforced at home.
5. Don't grade everything! Let students work in teams to grade or proofread work. Do this regularly so that it's a serious and continuous classroom activity.
6. Learning centers or stations for review, reinforcement, enrichment or exploration are perfect for beginning independent learners. Students don't have to decide what to study, when to study it, and how to study it, but they have to apply themselves in a self-instructional setting.
7. Students should have a chance now and then to set their own due date for an assignment. Give them a span of time, let them pick a date and then no excuses for late work!

RESPONSIBILITY RESOLVED?

Encouraging responsibility is serious business. Our success or failure is critical to the lives of the children we teach and to the survival of a healthy and productive society. In this new year, please include in your resolutions the following: "Be responsible for teaching responsibility."

Organizing the Middle/Junior High Laboratory Classroom

Terry Kwan

INTRODUCTION

Most of today's middle and junior high science educators are pretty well sold on a laboratory approach to teaching with concepts developed in carefully prepared sequences of investigations that the students are to perform for themselves. Instead of learning to memorize scores of facts from an encyclopedic science text or relying on the teacher for lectures and demonstrations, the student is increasingly urged into active participation. The laboratory program is an open invitation to see, to feel, to smell, and to do for oneself, to substitute hands-on experiences for vicarious ones.

It is easy to conjure up a picture of an ideal science class in operation. Small groups of students are randomly situated around the room working busily with numerous pieces of equipment. All are totally engrossed in their work leaving the teacher free to interact with kids individually. However, after a hectic day the picture may seem more like mass confusion, with all the students needing help at once, no one able to work the least bit independently, equipment broken or lost; all resulting in frustration for both students and teachers. The problem is not with the approach, nor with the lack of good intentions. What often happens is that ideals and theory get ahead of the practical problems of management.

For the new teacher, the task may seem even more overwhelming. One leaves methods and philosophy courses convinced that one should run a lab-oriented program involving active participation by students. Yet, faced with old classrooms, lack of the equipment package shown in the idealized curriculum, at least a hundred youngsters waiting to "try out" the new teacher, and an unbelievable amount of paperwork to do, it is very easy to put off doing the first lab and just do a little bit of talking and demonstrating. More often than not, the slight delay turns into a month or more, and when finally the first lab is undertaken, the confusion leaves the teacher vowing never to do another.

Managing a classroom laboratory with 30 or more active middle/junior high youngsters is a big job and requires not only good intentions, but careful planning and organization. Just as there is an orderly process by which one can develop a concept, there is likewise an orderly process by which one can develop an efficient and educationally wholesome, active laboratory classroom.

The intent of this article is to help put a little order into the organization of a junior high school laboratory classroom, to make the task somewhat less overwhelming, and thereby, to encourage beginning teachers to try the first lab with less apprehension and trauma. Included are ideas that have worked in poorly outfitted classrooms as well as ideally designed ones. As with most teaching techniques, these are a conglomerate of ideas stolen, adapted, and invented. Hopefully, you will feel free to adapt and rework them, adding inventions of your own.

CHOOSING THE FIRST ACTIVITY

The most common error in introducing middle/junior high school youngsters to laboratory activity is to assume too much. Particularly for new teachers recently completing thorough college science preparation with plenty of lab experience, there is a strong tendency to take many of the common laboratory techniques for granted. Remember that the average middle/junior high student's experience with laboratory activity is relatively limited in both depth and scope.

The first lab activity should be as simple as possible so that you can spend time establishing the routine and basic ground rules you wish followed, and so that you can get an idea of what the kids know or don't know and can or cannot do. In many cases, the student is really not aware of what constitutes an investigation or how one goes about logically solving a problem. For this reason, simple activities such as using red cabbage juice to produce color changes or observing a burning candle work well as an introduction. The manipulations called for are simple: using cabbage juice to produce color changes. The ideas taught are basic: how to recognize a problem, hypothesize, isolate variables, take observations, interpret data, and draw conclusions.

As you are going through the first investigation, teach basic techniques. Procedures like weighing and measuring, pouring and heating may be second nature to you, but are generally not well learned or remembered by the kids. The same is true for basic safety procedures. Do not presume that students will recognize what seem to you to be obvious safety hazards.

As students begin to do more lab activities, don't hesitate to review old techniques and procedures. Pertinent safety precautions should be reviewed every time a hazardous operation is performed and general techniques should be checked and reviewed if they haven't been used for awhile.

SEATING

The following factors should be considered in devising seating arrangements in the laboratory classroom:

1. Keep groups small. If possible, put only working partners or teams together. Avoid seating more than one team at a table and grouping too many tables together. This prevents teams from distracting each other and allows you to work with the teams individually without having to move or disturb neighboring teams.

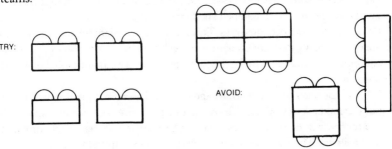

TRY:

AVOID:

2. Leave room for chairs to be pulled in and out. Make sure students do not bump into each other's chairs or tables when getting up to get a closer look at an experiment.
3. Avoid putting tables against walls or other tables so that students can work at their equipment from all sides, not just from in front.
4. Allow as much of a "buffer" zone as possible around each student group so that things which might boil over or pop out are not aimed directly at another team.
5. Keep aisles free and directed toward sinks and supply areas.
6. Keep student work tables away from sinks, supply areas, doors and other areas of heavy traffic.

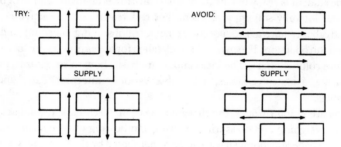

7. Remain flexible with furniture arrangements. If one arrangement doesn't work, change it. Even if you share the room with other teachers, remember that most furniture now is not bolted to the floor and without too much effort can be changed from period to period.

CLASSROOM STORAGE
Keep the following rules in mind for equipment storage:
1. Keep small objects in trays or shallow boxes below eye level for quick and easy checking.
2. Spread out equipment. Long shelves slightly below eye level are more convenient and safer than tall stacks of shelves confined to small areas. A longer storage area relieves congestion when students get and return equipment.
3. Store glassware in areas closest to sinks preferably on drying racks or open shelves.
4. Label shelves so students can easily find and return things. If larger objects are numbered, number the assigned shelf spaces also.
5. Put as much as you can into trays. Trays (cafeteria or planter), tote drawers, shoe boxes, or corrugated boxes with sides cut low are a real boon. These keep equipment in order and make it easy to pull out large quantities of materials at one time.
6. Label all the trays, shelves and storage areas of the room. You can use: (a) simple numbering or letter system; (b) name of equipment that belongs on the shelf; and (c) name or number of experiments that use the material or any combination of the above. Then put the same wording on all equipment.

PREPARATION OF CHEMICALS

If you are unfamiliar with a chemical you are about to use, check one of the standard chemical references for special properties and precautions. The following guidelines will help.

Dry Chemicals

1. Transfer materials from large bottles to small, wide mouth jars (baby food or jam jars) for classroom use.
2. Label all new bottles clearly. If the bottle is to be stored on a specific shelf or tray, put the shelf or tray number on the label also.
3. Keep bottles of chemicals less than one-half full. Students will waste less. If you have enough bottles and room to store them, make several small bottles for each chemical you plan to use heavily. Keep some of the bottles in storage to remove when needed.
4. Use wooden splints, tongue depressors, or plastic spoons for each dry chemical bottle to reduce contamination. Cut these implements down so they will fit inside the bottle. If it is not possible to store the dispensing instrument right in the bottle, try to get one spoon or scoopula for each chemical and label clearly.

Solutions

1. Polyethylene bottles of different sizes may be purchased for the preparation and storage of stock solutions. However, for the preparation of large volumes of solutions, it is much cheaper to recycle large plastic bottles such as those in which cider, windshield washer fluid, and fabric softener come. Old bleach bottles also work, but are not as convenient because they are opaque. Have students donate empty plastic bottles from home but make sure they bring the caps also. If you can obtain a number of the same kind of bottle, transfer measured volumes to graduate one bottle, then simply stand it next to the others to mark all the rest. For the preparation of most stock solutions, gradations made this way are accurate enough and cut down greatly on preparation time.
2. Before preparing a solution, check the directions and the purpose of the solution. Determine how quantitative you must be in your preparation. You can be less accurate if the solution called for is to be saturated (e.g., limewater) or is to be used merely to show the presence of some substance (e.g., barium chloride to test for sulfate or tincture of iodine to test for starch) or is intended only to demonstrate gross reaction (e.g., lead nitrate and potassium iodide to show precipitation). In the latter cases, you can shortcut by adding enough reagent to tip rather than exactly balance the scale. Then make a note of how many scoopsful approximate the correct weight and label such information on the stock bottle for subsequent use.
3. There are times when accuracy is a must. Make the solution exactly the first time and every time. This is essential for solutions that are used for any type of titration or for experiments requiring students to obtain quantitative results. It is best to follow exact measurements in preparing solutions with more than one

component (e.g., Nessler's Reagent). Cost of the chemicals is also a factor. Preparation of indicator solutions requires more prudence than the preparation of sodium chloride or magnesium sulfate solutions.

4. If the chemicals happen to come in small quantities, and you have an unopened bottle, save some time by taking into account the weight of the full bottle. For instance, if you need 500 grams of a substance which comes in 1 lb. bottles, use an unopened bottle without weighing and just add another 46 grams from another bottle. (This is not a totally accurate procedure and should not be used for preparation of quantitative reagents).

5. In the preparation of saturated solutions, decanting is often more convenient than filtering large quantities of solution. Remember not to shake up the stock bottles before transferring to bottles for classroom use and you can use the excess from old stock to make new stock.

6. Check the condition of your tap water before preparing solutions. If the water is relatively mineral free, and the pipes don't add their own special seasoning, you may be able to make most solutions with ordinary tap water even though the directions call for distilled. It's worth the time to prepare a small sample solution to see if tap water will work before going through the trouble of ordering and trying to store 50 gallons of distilled water or installing a deionizer. On the other hand, you may find the tap water is so bad, you will have to do everything in distilled or deionized water, even if the "recipe" doesn't specify it.

7. Once you have prepared a stock solution, be sure it is properly labeled. This may be done with marker or masking tape, but first make sure there is no old labeling left on the bottle. Make sure that new labeling is not merely obscuring old labeling.

General Procedures for Preparing Chemicals

1. After preparing an experiment or fresh stock solutions, test the materials to avoid unhappy surprises when 30 students are waiting to do an experiment.

2. Reserve red labeling for safety precautions and hazard warnings.

3. Date chemicals when they are received or prepared. Date the chemical bottles again when they are opened for the first time and indicate with a mark the fill line of the new bottle. This allows you to determine how fast you are using them.

PREPARING FOR A LAB

If most of your equipment is stored on open shelves and students are familiar with the locations, you may be able to run labs without a lot of special setting up. However, you can also put things out in a central supply area for the particular exercise being done. In setting up a central supply table, keep in mind the following guidelines:

1. List all the materials that will be needed for the lab.

2. Gather trays, tote drawers, or shallow boxes for each type of equipment needed (cafeteria trays and shoe boxes are appropriate).

3. Label each tray or box with the name of the equipment that is to be kept in it.

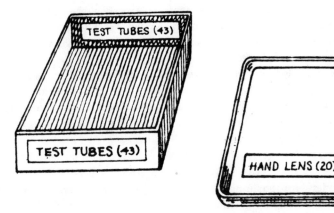

4. Count out the pieces of equipment needed. Write the number of articles in the tray on the tray label. If you are simply pulling a prelabeled tray from the shelf, you can count out just the pieces needed and store the spares somewhere else or simply use the whole tray.

It is better to have an accurate count of materials that easily disappear than to put out a whole trayful. Check your materials after the experiment before the class leaves the room.

LAB TEAMS

Assign numbers to the lab teams either permanently or for each lab depending on how often you intend to switch partners. Use these numbers to assign special tasks or equipment. This way you can make assignments with a master list of only 10 or 20 numbers rather than trying to keep track of 150 or 200 separate student assignments.

Assign a special task to each team according to team number. Much of this can be special jobs to help speed clean-up. Post a list of team assignments conspicuously in the room so that you and the students can refer to it quickly at any time.

1. Check and refill alcohol burners.
2. Sink clean-up.
3. Demonstration or supply table clean-up.
4. Check floors for paper and stray equipment.
5. Check equipment shelves for proper return of all trays.
6. Collect and store unfinished projects for the next session. (Check to see that each piece is clearly labeled.)
7. Check and refill solution and chemical bottles.
8. Count equipment that has been set out in special numbers.

Other assigned tasks can be custodianship for special or easily misplaced equipment such as safety glasses; balances and weight sets for balances; books (texts, lab manuals, instruction sheets, and lab reports); dissecting kits; and microscopes. This equipment should be numbered and the numbers should appear both on the equipment and on the shelf space or hook where it is to be stored.

If there are full class sets of the equipment, students should be instructed to use only the piece that corresponds to their team number. If each team uses more than one piece of the same equipment (e.g., safety glasses), then number with the team number followed by A, B, C, etc.

When there are only a few pieces of the equipment (not enough to assign one to each team), set up a signout system and make one team responsible for the item. Number or letter the equipment, and provide signout sheets. The team in charge of the equipment is responsible for signing it out and giving a final accounting at the end of the period.

SAFETY PROCEDURES

1. Keep the rules short and simple. This makes them easy for students to remember and easier for the teacher to enforce.
2. Teachers and guests should follow the safety rules just as carefully as the students. Junior high and middle school students tend to learn safety more by imitation and repetition than by logic. Therefore, it is extremely important that the teacher get into the habit of following safety rules consistently, even when students are not around.
3. Label everything clearly. Reserve red for safety cautions.
4. Check the properties of unfamiliar reagents in a good reference. Teach your students how to use standard reference manuals as well and get them in the habit of using them.
5. Give a general lab safety lesson as early as possible. Point out locations of exits and safety equipment (fire extinguishers, showers, fume hoods, etc.) and give instruction on emergency procedure.
6. Special safety rules such as instruction on the handling of acids are much more effective when taught just prior to use. Review pertinent general rules and special safety instruction immediately before each lab involving hazards.
7. Have the students write their own copies of the safety rules and insist that these be brought to all lab classes. When special techniques are taught, the accompanying safety rules should be added to the original list.
8. Establish a signal to get immediate attention from the whole class. Use a whistle, bell, buzzer, or flick the lights. Make it clear that the signal means all activity is to come to an immediate stop.
9. Enforce the safety rules strictly and consistently. Contact parents directly and immediately in cases of habitual or deliberate disregard for safety regulations.

IN THE LAB

Some general points to keep in mind while working with students in the lab include the following:

1. Keep moving. Don't spend all or most of your time with one or two groups. If you haven't changed areas in 5 minutes, you are probably so wrapped up in the team with which you are working that you don't really know what the rest of the class is really doing.

2. Keep listening. Even when working individually with students or teams, listen to what is going on elsewhere at the same time.
3. Make use of mirrors, windows, and other reflecting surfaces to check behind and around you while working where your direct view is obstructed. No matter where you are in the room, keep eyes and ears open for signals from everywhere else.
4. Encourage students to help each other. Instead of answering each question several times, refer students to other students whom you helped with the same problem.
5. Respond to quiet calls for help before noisy tantrums.
6. Encourage use of reference materials for factual information.
7. Establish a signal to get immediate full class attention.
8. STAY CALM!

BREAKAGE

In a working lab, it is inevitable that things break. This usually occurs with an audible crash followed by dead silence or possibly a cheer as the class waits to observe the teacher's reaction. Regardless of the reason for the accident, a good immediate response is to quietly give instructions to clean up quickly without further disruption. This gives the teacher time to determine the cause of the breakage and decide what to do about it.

Different schools have their own rules about breakage fees, so it is best to check the general procedure first. One method that has worked well is to charge the student the current cost of the item if it is broken because of carelessness and double the cost if it is broken on purpose or while doing something specifically restricted.

In any case, keep a record of all the items that are broken along with date and name of the student who broke. You may find some consistent patterns and want to take some time to check on the technique of students habitually breaking things or change a procedure if a lot of children keep having similar accidents.

CLEANUP

Cleanup can make or break a laboratory program. It is imperative that the room be cleaned up and put back in order at the end of each period, not just once at the end of the day or when you can no longer stand the mess. Classes entering a messy lab tend to work more sloppily and leave the lab in worse shape at the end of the period. A number of factors contribute to efficient and relatively stress-free cleanup periods:
1. Insist on proper cleanup from the very first lab. Don't wait until the sloppiness obstructs progress. Continue to check cleanup in every lab period, not just intermittently.
2. Make each person responsible for his or her own area and materials but don't hesitate to ask students to help each other as well. Likewise help them and ask that they help you.
3. Assign individuals or teams to take charge of common areas and to check on the return of various items.

4. Scan common areas such as sink and supply tables several times during the period. If things are unsatisfactory, stop the whole class right then and have the mess cleaned up before allowing anyone to continue regular work.
5. Store glassware on drying racks or open shelves. Let the natural process of evaporation take care of drying. This saves time and paper towels.
6. Plan for cleanup time in the regular lesson schedule. Don't just squeeze it in between the dismissal bell and the next class. Initially, this may take 10 to 15 minutes, but time can be shortened to less than five minutes in a lab where materials are clean and easily located. Give a warning 1-5 minutes before cleanup time so students can wind up their experiments or get them set to store overnight. When cleanup time arrives, stop all lab work and get everyone to straighten things up and put things away.
7. Use plenty of labeling. Label shelves and materials, trays and bottles, so students can tell where to put things even after forgetting where they got them.
8. Have everyone return to seats after cleanup. Then take a minute to scan common areas, desks, lab benches, sinks and equipment. Don't dismiss anyone until all is in order.
9. Don't forget the compliments. If things look good or cleanup was quick and efficient, reward the students by letting them know you noticed.

WASTE DISPOSAL

For ecological as well as economic reasons, consideration should be given to waste disposal and the possibilities of recycling. Solid wastes are usually the most troublesome, particularly if they are also wet and only partially congealed. If the material is relatively dense, a pail or deep container in the sink works well. Students can be instructed to dump and rinse directly into the pail where the solids can be collected and prevented from stopping the drain.

Thought should also be given to the possible reuse of materials. In some of the new science programs, many of the solutions can be reused, even after they have been diluted or slightly contaminated. Remember to keep separate containers for fresh stock and contaminated stock. Sometimes the end products of one experiment are used as reactants for another experiment.

Provide separate waste containers for broken glass, used matches, and organic wastes. As with everything else, mark waste disposal containers clearly and place them where students are most likely to dump materials, near the sink or supply tables.

IMPROVISING EQUIPMENT

Improvising equipment can be both challenging and satisfying. It is a concrete way to boost ecology and demonstrates that good science does not require stainless steel laboratories with rows of flawless test tubes. Improvisation may trim quite a bit from a tight science budget and be a lifesaver if you just can't find what you need. For example, test tube racks may be improvised by cutting holes in shoe boxes or milk cartons or by drilling holes in a piece of wood.

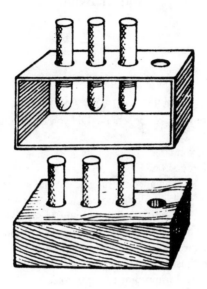

Students are quite good at improvising equipment. Often they are able to construct simple devices that perform the same functions as more expensive pieces of specialized equipment simply because they see the problem first and not the classical apparatus. Good sources of ideas, help, and material are other science teachers, custodians, the cafeteria staff, and shop teachers. Some of their clutter may be just what you need.

Good luck with your next lab. Try to relax and enjoy it!

HANDBOOKS

Some good standard references for the laboratory classroom are:

Handbook of Chemistry and Physics, Robert C. Weast, ed. The Chemical Rubber Co. Press, Cleveland, Ohio (yearly).

The Merck Index, Paul G. Stecher, ed. Merck & Co., Inc., Rahway, N.J. 1976.

Handbook of Nature Study, Anna Botsford Comstock, Comstock Publishing Co., Inc., Ithaca, N.Y. 1939.

Safety in the Secondary Science Classroom. National Science Teachers Association, Washington, D.C. 1978 (rev. 1983).

Laboratory Waste Disposal Manual. Manufacturing Chemists Association, Washington, D.C. 1969 (rev. 1973).

Creativity—Nurture and Stimulation

Rodger Bybee

MARY, MELVIN AND JOHN

"Mary, why are you late for school? Did you leave home on time?"

"Yes, I did."

"Then why are you late?"

"I guess I walk too slow."

"But I saw you looking at something across the street."

"Oh yes! I was walking along looking at the sidewalk when I saw moss growing in the cracks. I started looking around to see all the places I could find moss. You should have seen some of the places I found it—on a brick wall, under a tree in a garden, on the street by the curb."

"But Mary, we must start school on time."

"Yes, but it seemed important to me to look."

"Perhaps it was, Mary, but it's time to start class."

Melvin was staring out the window at the snow.

"Are you daydreaming, Melvin? We're talking about community helpers. Were you thinking about helpers, Melvin?"

"Yes, I was helping track down a giant Snowflake. The story is 'Melvin and the Monster Snowflake.' I was sent to capture the Monster Snowflake, but whenever I got close, it would melt and become invisible; the white would go away. Then the Snowflake, disguised as water, would go somewhere else and reappear as a snowflake. I was having a hard time because the Snowflake would change into water and become invisible, and when it came back it would be different. All snowflakes are different, you know."

"That's an interesting story Melvin, but it really isn't related to what we're studying."

John was wandering around the classroom, messing with various objects, distracting other children as he walked around.

"John, what are you doing?"

"My lunch is gone."

"Didn't you leave it in your desk?"

"Yes, but it's gone."

"Where is it?"

"I was wondering the same thing."

Art by Robyn Johnson-Ross

Are these children's behaviors creative or disruptive? Some will think the children are inquisitive, original, unique, and bold. They will see the children as being creative. Others may consider the children neglectful, inattentive, troublesome, even disobedient. Still others will decide some of the behaviors are creative and others are disruptive. This ambiguity is intentional. Children's creative behavior is not always well-defined when considered in the context of the teacher's perceptions, the classroom, the curriculum, and the administration.

Creativity is one of the paradoxical issues in American education. It is valued, cherished, and recognized as an important goal. Yet in actual practice, creative potential is seldom actualized. In a time of concern for the basics, it is also important to consider children's creativity. Individual development is a basic goal of education. Much research on creativity supports a position that the creative process is an important part of each person. We should, then, accept creativity as important and work to develop it during the formal educational process.

Knowledge of your own creativity will help in appreciating creativity in others. Try some of the experiences in the box. Try them alone and with your class.

Experiencing Creativity

These activities are designed to help an individual realize some of his or her own creativity. They don't include all aspects of creativity nor will they insure your becoming a more creative person. Experiencing creativity takes a type of giving up of oneself to the process. These activities can provide a catalyst.

Unique in the Common

Look around. Can you see something unique in a common object? Are there colors and relationships among shapes you haven't seen before? What about patterns of positive and negative space? Watch a sunset, a child at play, look at the buildings on your way home. Try to find something uncommon in a common place or thing.

Past and Future

Take some deep breaths. Sit back, relax, close your eyes. Imagine your favorite flower. In your imagination, stare at the flower. Give yourself up to your thoughts.

Appreciation and Joy

Do you have a picture or pictures of somebody close to you? Take out your picture(s). Think about the person, experiencing the freshness of appreciation and enjoyment this person brings to you.

Awareness and Insight

Many people have someplace that is very special. In this place, proprietary milieu, we are at peace with ourselves. Facades are down. There is no role playing. Where is this place for you? Is it at home, out-of-doors? Are you alone or with someone? What are you doing? What is going on around you?

Changing Perceptions

Imagine being where you are now and only 5 cm tall. What does the world look like? Now imagine you are 3 m tall. How do your perceptions change? What does the world look like now?

Fantasy

Join the story of "Melvin and the Monster Snowflake." Be the snowflake. You can melt, disguise yourself as another snowflake, freeze, evaporate, and sublimate. Where would you go? What would you do to get away from Melvin?

Creativity is sometimes defined as a product whether it be a new idea, a painting, or a story. Creativity is also an internal process made up of puzzlement about something, thought about the problem, an incubation period, illumination, and finally verification or refutation of the solution. Both process and product must be considered in the definition. An act, such as creativity, needs reference to an object. One characteristic of the creative process is directedness. The process results in something, an object, an idea, even an unspecifiable thought. To reverse this, if creativity is only the product how did the product come to be? These ideas are important in recognizing and developing creativity. Both process and product must be considered. In the end it is the child or adult who does the creating.

RECOGNIZING CREATIVITY

It is difficult to observe a single act or behavior in a short period and say whether it is creative or not. The tendency to reduce and analyze in an attempt to understand often leads to trouble, especially in areas such as creativity. Teachers can observe students in their classes over some length of time. Bringing together a holistic picture of children in light of the characteristics discussed is a better way to view classroom creativity. I will cite one imaginary child, Alfred, as a continuous example to allow an image of a creative person to form in the reader's mind.

Openness is a fundamental characteristic of a creative person. These people are comfortable in a position of ambiguity; at these times many inputs that catalyze new ideas and different ways of thinking about old ideas are realized. Jean Piaget's (10)[1] discussion of disequilibrium and the subsequent process of equilibration and John Dewey's (2) discussion of thinking that results from experience and problems are both processes by which ideas are considered, changed, and contribute to growth.

Being open to suggestions provides opportunity for creative thinking. Alfred could take a simple idea and stretch, expand, and modify it into a more elegant idea. Part of this type of creative thinking is use of imagination.

For children like Alfred, all teachers need to do is ask questions such as, "What if you were . . ." "What would happen if . . . ?" These questions bring forth continuous response that slowly drifts off to fantasy land. Sometimes the questions do not have to be asked, as in the opening example of Melvin. Most teachers recognize imagination, fantasy, and intellectual playfulness.

So far, creativeness has been talked about as inspiration, illumination, or working through inspiration. Melvin, for example, had an inspiration for a story about a monster snowflake. The difference between this idea and the final story is persistence, dedication, a willingness to work, and continued enthusiasm for the idea.

Fluency, flexibility, and originality are likewise traits of creativity. When asked an openended question such as "How many ways could you use a plastic spoon?" Alfred could produce a continuous flow of ideas: to eat with, to launch paper missiles with, to make noise with, to melt. Fluency is generating ideas or responses relevant to a particular question.

---

[1] See References.

53

"Can you think of different uses for magnets?" Alfred could produce unique ideas such as holding false teeth or a wig in place. Flexibility in thought is changing of categories, varying production of ideas to let unique ideas emerge.

"Can you think of a new kind of alarm clock?" Originality, thinking in novel or unique ways, and clever ideas are all recognizable qualities of creative children. Alfred was always coming up with unexpected responses, wild ideas, and unusual ways of seeing the familiar. For an alarm clock, he designed an elaborate computerized system with many pleasant experiences to awaken the sleeper, such as the smell of fresh coffee, the sound of soft music, the voice of a friend, vibrations in the bed. The pleasant experience could be programmed by the person who bought the clock. One would be randomly selected each morning by the computer, so the person never knew what to expect, but would always be pleasantly awakened. But "alarm clock" is not a good name for his device, since it is associated with warning or danger. Can you think of a name that better describes Alfred's clock?

Creative people also show courage, complexity, and curiosity. Mary's response to why she was late, "It seemed important to me," typifies the self-assertive, confident student. Alfred was not afraid to guess or expose his ideas to criticism. This pioneering, risk-taking spirit often put him in positions where he stood alone from his peers. Seemingly, this did not bother him. He was not influenced by the group; he had the courage to stand up for his ideas. Alfred's behavior also showed complexity. He was introspective, immersed in his thoughts and ideas. His courage to the outer world was complemented by the examination of his inner world.

Mary's curiosity caused her lateness for school. Stopping to take a closer look, preoccupation with problems, following a hunch just to see what happens, are all important to creativity. It is as though Mary were following Rilke's advice to a young poet, "Try to love the *questions themselves*." (11)

Fluency, flexibility, originality of ideas, openness to experience, courage, and imagination are characteristics all children exhibit to some degree. Recognizing them as creative is an individual judgment. What I have described is not the special talent *creativity*; it is creativity you can see in students everyday. Teachers should recognize creativity's primary processes; spontaneity, insight, fantasy, originality. If creativity's early processes are accepted, the secondary processes—the working through, the testing, and finishing the product—are likely to occur.

ACCEPTING CREATIVITY

Were the children in the anecdotes creative or disruptive? Obviously, that is the wrong question to ask. All the children showed some creative behavior that also caused disruption in their classes. The degree to which a student's behavior is seen as creative depends on the teacher's recognizing and accepting creativity as an educational goal. Children's behaviors must be looked at in the larger context of education. John may have been disruptive. Still, he shows elements of individual creativity. What are they?

Acceptance is the heart of the matter for classroom teachers concerned about creativity. Teachers who, for the most part, recognize creativity in their classrooms, sometimes do not accept and value it. The creative child is seen as maladjusted, a misfit, out of the mainstream. A study by Torrance asked teachers to note how far they would encourage or discourage isolated characteristics. Creative behaviors generally ranked low. (12)

Calvin Taylor has used a unique way of approaching this problem: *Design an educational environment that stifles creativity*.[2] Sadly, the description paints a fairly accurate picture of too many classrooms. Included are conformity in lessons, compliance, restriction, punishment for creative behavior, appeal to authority, "cookbook" approaches, emphasis on answers, intolerance of mistakes, suppression.

What do we mean by acceptance? *All* behavior in a classroom is not acceptable. If Alfred ran around banging chairs, disrupting the class, he is not being "creative." However, teachers can decide to accept creativity as a purpose of education and develop an atmosphere for encouraging creativity in the classroom.

DEVELOPING CREATIVITY

What type of classroom best nurtures creativity? A rich, stimulating classroom environment is warm and exciting and offers elements conducive to creative thought—bulletin boards, colors, books, plants, animals, blocks, interest centers, and tools that invite curiosity and act as catalysts for creativity. Such an atmosphere encourages children's spontaneous and original expression. The stimulating environment is also characterized by the warm, trusting interpersonal relationship existing between teacher and students. Students realize the teacher is interested in their ideas, and accepts and encourages creative ideas.

CREATIVE LEARNING ACTIVITIES

Activities to stimulate creativity should have a base in reading, art, language, science, and social studies lessons. Creativity should be an extension or sequence within the lessons. As a group, children should have opportunity to inquire, question, search, forecast, guess, hypothesize, and abstract during the lessons without fear of being penalized for wrong answers. Teachers should ask openended questions and present unsolved problems, puzzles, and brain teasers. Some activities should encourage imaginative, fictional thinking. Gray offers ideas for encouraging creativity. (4,5)

TIME FOR CREATIVITY

Set aside a time to be used exclusively for development of creative activities. While other studies would be involved, their emphasis would be secondary. Having a special time for creativity does not imply it cannot occur at other times. I am talking about a special time when any creative behavior, within limits, is acceptable.

First, introduce and practice skills and techniques of creative thinking. Group activities such as brainstorming, synectics (3), making up stories, and discussing

---

[2] Calvin Taylor used this activity at a creativity workshop conducted at the University of Utah.

mythical problems could be activities. During these times spontaneous expression in movement, drama, art or speech, fantasy, and speculation would be encouraged. (1, 6, 7, 13) Finally, recognize the importance of private time. Students need time to think, study, and reflect.

All students are creative, but all students' behavior is not creative. Through observation and careful listening you can identify the creative talents of your children. Accept creativity. Be willing to work toward actualization of children's creative potential. It takes "courage to create." (9) This is true for students—and for everyone, for that matter. It takes courage to change perceptions of student behavior and accept creativity, and to try to develop it in our teaching and students.

REFERENCES

1. Bybee, Rodger W. "Creativity, Children, and Elementary Science." *Science and Children*, 9:22-26; March 1972.
2. Dewey, John. *Democracy and Education*. The Free Press, New York City, 1966. (See Chapter 11 especially.)
3. Gordon, William J. *Synectics: The Development of Creative Capacity*. Macmillan, Inc., New York City, 1968.
4. Gray, Wanda. "Creativity Doesn't Just Happen." *Learning*: 9-12; January 1973.
5. Gray, Wanda. "Uncommon Learning from Common Experience." *Learning*: 30-32; March 1973.
6. McCormack, Alan J. and Gary Doi. "Creativity Is A Bunch of Junk." *Science and Children*, 10:9-12; September 1972.
7. McCormack, Alan J. and Gary Doi. "Creatoons." *The Teacher*:92; January 1974.
8. McCormack, Alan J. and Gary Doi. "Wanted." *The Teacher*:76; February 1974.
9. May, Rollo. "On the Courage to Create." *Media and Methods*:15-61; May-June 1974.
10. Piaget, Jean. *Origins of Intelligence in Children*. Margaret Cook, tr., International Universities Press, Inc., New York City, 1966.
11. Rilke, Rainer M. *Letters to a Young Poet*. W.W. Norton & Co., Inc., New York City, 1963.
12. Torrance, E. Paul. *Guiding Creative Talent*. R.E. Krieger Publishing Co., Inc., Huntington, New York, 1962.
13. Wayman, Joseph. "The Creative Child—What You Can Do." *The Teacher*:26-28; March 1973.

Rating Your Individualized Program

James A. Shymansky

The push toward individualization in recent years has been felt in all areas of education, especially in science. Administrators and teachers often feel compelled to individualize their programs—or at least to claim that they have done so—to avoid being ostracized or considered old-fashioned. Why the big push? Does evidence show that instruction is improved when it is individualized? This question merits a long, hard look. Individualized science programs have been around in one form or another for about 15 years, so the question can be debated.

The major rationale for individualizing instruction is clear. Students will do better when instruction is tailored to meet individual needs. The teacher's role also seems clear. The teacher should create an environment in which all students can realize their individual potential. The technique is often referred to as "facilitating" student learning. But what does facilitating look like? How does facilitating or individualizing instruction differ from just plain teaching? Depending on whom you ask, the answers to these questions vary greatly.

Unfortunately, most research studies of individualization in science instruction tend to gloss over what the teacher does or doesn't do to effect the process. Occasionally there is casual mention that the teacher should move from student to student, that the teacher should ask open-ended questions, or that students should appear to be working on their own. But for teachers who want to start an individualized program, these observations offer little help. Unfortunately, without guidance, the teacher may develop misconceptions about individualization in the classroom and what it can or should be.

TEACHER'S ROLE

Let's look at the teacher's role and planning as important elements of individualizing science instruction. If teachers don't understand what their own roles in an individualized program are or if they don't properly plan activities that complement individualization, instruction may be less effective in meeting pupils' needs and end up as *less* personalized than in the more traditional large group setting. In one study, data concerning individualization in junior high school science programs were gathered. (2)* The purpose of this study, done at the request of teachers and school administrators, was to provide a profile of each school's science instruction in terms of kinds of teaching materials and methods being used. In the school using a so-called individualized approach to teaching science, some startling observations were made. Four teachers were observed spending up to 78 percent of inclass time managing the instructional program—checking assignments, recording student

*See References

selection of activities, administering pretests, posttests, makeup tests, and performing clerical duties. Little or no time was spent with pupils in an individualized setting to accomplish the goals of the science of the activities. One of the major strengths of an individualized program is that students receive more personal attention from the teacher through small group interactions. The individualized classrooms in this study were not meeting this criterion.

More disturbing than the large amount of time spent by teachers on management tasks was the fact that the students were caught up in the management aspects of instruction as well. Although no formal data were collected on how student time was spent in these classrooms, the observers' informal written comments noted that students spent as little as five minutes of the 45-minute class on science-related activities. As might be expected from the previously mentioned teacher profiles, students spent much time waiting in line to check out activities with the teacher, handing in assignments, or waiting to use certain equipment.

This situation is probably not that different from other individualized science programs throughout the country. On the surface, the programs appear good. Students are working on their own projects or contracts at their own rates. Many instructional media are being used. Major ingredients for good instruction are there, but there is one serious deficiency—the teacher and the teacher's role. Somehow the teachers and the roles they play got lost in the shuffle. Instead of more frequent and meaningful interactions between teachers and students, these classrooms are caught up in management and mechanical activity.

Individualization is *not* a panacea. It is possible, in fact, that the quality of teacher-student interactions and the overall instructional quality may diminish. Pitfalls exist. So do opportunities for learning *improvement*. But giving up and reverting to large group lectures where science is taught by recitation and an occasional laboratory experience is not an acceptable alternative. There *are* problems with individualizing science instruction, but this does not mean that the idea should be discarded. The rationale behind individualization is still valid. The challenge is to make individualism a real part of the classroom and to make it more effective than other instructional modes. Until now, this challenge has been largely met at the materials level. The next step is to meet the challenge at the teacher and instructional level.

WHAT TEACHERS CAN DO

What can teachers do to improve their individualization efforts? "Start with one practical step and work toward the ideal." (1) Sound advice, but there is a second part. Every so often, assess where you are in the journey. By adding the assessment component, chances are less that you will lose sight of the reasons for wanting to individualize in the first place. Chances are greater that you will not stop short of your goal. The decrease in one-to-one teacher-student contacts due to a preoccupation with management aspects of individualization is the first pitfall. Self-pacing can be a second pitfall. The idea of students working at their own rate started out as a step toward individualization for many classroom teachers. But, in fact, self-pacing too often becomes an end in itself. Even though it has taken on this status in many schools, self-pacing is not individualization. Think, for a moment, about the difference. Is self-pacing an aspect of individualizing? What does research suggest as a set of guidelines that teachers can follow in an attempt to individualize? Here are some suggestions to consider:

1. *Severing* ties and total dependence on a single textbook, laboratory manual, or program. There are many resources available. Increasing the number of sources of activities and ideas increases opportunities for students to make decisions about what will be learned and how it will be learned. This is a key factor in individualization.

2. *Varying* the instructional modes available to students, making sure to offer several different ones simultaneously. For example, provide science learning centers that offer opportunities for individual selection and design of activities. Access individualized work with core activities and offer options for student-designed excursions. Involve students in long-term and short-term projects. Encourage small-group activities with opportunities for student-initiated work. These are all ways to move instruction toward the individualized end of the continuum. A key factor in all of these is to allow students to take part in determining objectives.

3. *Moving around.* Make an effort to spend time working with individual students and small groups. Spend less time teaching the group as a whole.

4. *Streamlining* your record-keeping system. This will minimize the amount of class time you and your students spend checking materials and assignments.

5. *Monitoring* your activity and the activity of individual students periodically. Find out how much time you and your students spend in productive, sciencing activity and how much time you spend on program mechanics and administration. Audiotapes of class activity can provide a good picture of productivity. Daily student logs are also a good source of this information.

6. *Examining*, reexamining, and evaluating your role. You should be teaching differently in an individualized setting. Don't be concerned if you aren't the center of attention. That's the way it should be.

Here is a system for monitoring your individualization efforts. Where do *you* stand?

1. Is your instruction based on one textbook and/or laboratory manual?
   ☐ No - score 1   ☐ Yes - score 0

2. In class today, were different students learning through different media?
   ☐ Yes - score 1   ☐ No - score 0

3. Were students given the option of working on different topics or activities?
   ☐ Yes - score 1   ☐ No - score 0 (Skip to No. 5)

4. Who designed the activities that students worked on?
   ☐ Student - score 1   ☐ Teacher - score 0

5. Did you spend more time interacting with individual students or small groups of less than six than with large groups?
   ☐ Yes - score 1 (go to No. 6)   ☐ No - score 0 (stop)

6. Did you spend more time today checking on materials, checking and making assignments, and grading work than you did working with students on the science activity, individually, in small groups, and large groups combined?
   ☐ No - score 1   ☐ Yes - score 0

Add up your scores. If you got six points, your science program is individualized. You've got a handle on the basics. Now refine other efforts such as questioning skills. If your score is three to five, you are headed in the right direction and are ready to take the next steps. If your score is less than three, yet you think you have an individualized program, you need to take a closer look. That's nothing more than you'd expect your students to do in the event they too achieved less.

REFERENCES
1. Johnson, P. C. "Individualized Teaching and Learning." *The Science Teacher*. 41:20-22; September 1974.
2. Shymansky, J. A. "Assessing Teacher Performance in the Classroom: Pattern Analysis Applied to Interaction Data." *Studies in Educational Evaluation*. 4:99-106; 1978.

Organizing an Outdoor Education Field Trip For Junior High Students

Pierce F. McCabe
Gail Novy Kleisner

INITIAL PLANNING

In August of 1976, two teachers from Godwin Junior High, Cicero, Illinois, visited the Cloverleaf Girl Scout Camp near Sheridan, Illinois. They were immediately struck with the idea of an outdoor educational program for the eighth-grade students of their school. They visualized an overnight camping trip during the following spring.

When they returned to school in September, they talked to fellow staff members to gain support for the trip. They explained that staff participation in such a program would require a great deal of time both before and during the trip—time spent preparing lesson plans, visiting the camp, and spending several nights with the pupils. Three teachers and the assistant principal agreed to try such a program. Thus, a team of six teachers was formed who took responsibility for planning, coordinating, and teaching classes on the field trip. The team was made up of three science teachers, a physical education instructor, a social studies teacher, and a language arts teacher. Most had had some camping experience and one teacher had extensive first aid training.

The next step was to approach the administration both at the school and at the district level for obtaining approval. After having secured tentative approval from the school administration, formal approval was sought and obtained from the Girl Scout Board as well as from the district administration.

OBJECTIVES

As a starting point, the six teachers began the task of outlining the outdoor program. Using several books as guides on outdoor education, the planners developed program objectives, in-school orientation, program activities, and in-school followup.

The overall program objectives included the following:

- To enhance science education
- To enhance conservation education
- To enhance outdoor recreation
- To enhance camping knowledge
- To enhance environmental education.

In-school orientation included activities in each discipline:

Science: building a terrarium, diagraming food chains, identifying rock types, learning how to use a hand level, and using classroom charts to identify major constellations.

Physical Education: learning proper outdoor dress, practicing outdoor safety, and learning how to make and pack a bedroll.

Social Studies: reviewing map skills, learning how to use a compass, and discussing man's use and misuse of the environment.

Language Arts: reviewing letter writing skills, reviewing notetaking, learning proper labeling, and discussing listening skills.

Mathematics: using the metric system of measurement, learning to figure one's own pace, learning estimating skills, and figuring the finances of the trip.

Home Economics: learning proper menu planning for the trip, as well as outdoor tips on cooking, and proper table serving techniques.

MEETING WITH PARENTS

In February, the trip was first mentioned to parents, but only in general terms. The teachers met with the parents in early May to give them the final plans, equipment list, permission slips and emergency slips (signed, if possible, at this time). Parents were instructed on the correct way to make and pack a bedroll and the proper way to pack. This participation resulted in parental appreciation of the need to eliminate some supplies.

DIVIDING GROUPS

In order to keep the adult-pupil ratio as low as possible and to facilitate housing accommodations, it was decided to divide the students into two groups with the boys going to camp on Monday and Tuesday, and the girls going on Thursday and Friday. Those remaining behind were expected to attend school and were supervised by remaining school personnel. Regular classes were held for all students on Wednesday.

Before leaving for camp, two alphabetical lists, one of boys and one of girls, were compiled. The lists contained important data taken from the permission slips: name, address, address and phone number where parent could be reached in an emergency, and any medication being brought to camp or additional parental comments. The list was mimeographed and distributed to administrative personnel remaining in town as well as faculty members participating in the trip. (Only one emergency occurred when a parent needed to be contacted, and the emergency list proved invaluable.)

MENUS

Students were instructed in home economics class about menu planning, cost, and quantity. With the estimates of transportation and food, the cost of the trip was set at $10 per student, which included $.50 per student for use of the campground.

Students voted on the menus for the three meals (supper the first day and breakfast and lunch the second day). They dined on the following:

First Day:

Snack at 3:00 - apple

Supper - sloppy joe on bun, salad, banana pudding, potato chips, milk

Snack at campfire - "s'mores"

Second Day:

Breakfast - orange juice, bacon, pancakes, milk

Lunch - hot dogs, potato chips, lemonade, carrot and celery sticks

Snack before going home - donuts, cookies, milk or lemonade

All food was purchased by a faculty member and students. It was taken to the camp prior to the trip and refrigerated and stored.

TEACHER PREPARATION AND EQUIPMENT

Prior to the trip itself, the teachers made two or three trips out to the camp. Armed with maps of the area, they hiked around the camp to check on where they were to teach, set up an obstacle course for the physical education classes, and, in general, familiarized themselves with the area where they would be camping. They knew that some of the girls had been out to the camp as members of the Scouts, and wanted to make sure that they knew the layout as well as the girls did.

The staff began to secure the necessary equipment after having seen the camp. One of the hardest items to obtain was a long sturdy rope used for climbing, which was eventually borrowed from the Chicago Fire Department. A horn was secured to use in announcing the end of each class. (The horn was also used to awaken the pupils in the mornings and to call the group together for any announcements. Many students listed the horn as the thing they liked least about the trip.) Other items secured for the trip which were not on the students' equipment list included compasses, meter sticks, gallon jars (obtained from the cooks in the cafeteria), a first aid kit, watches, whistles, alarm clock, flashlights, knives, cameras, film, and walkie-talkies.

Teachers began preparing students for the trip in the classroom by discussing what they would be doing and what they would have to know for the trip. In science, students worked with various charts for plant and tree identification. In P.E. class, they learned how to make a bedroll and how to pack all of their gear inside of it.

Each teacher who participated in the trip also had to prepare lesson plans for the students who remained behind. These lesson plans dealt with items that related to the environment, pollution, conservation, and other subjects which were closely tied to the trip itself.

CAMP SCHEDULE

When they arrived at the camp, the students unloaded their bedrolls and chose their sleeping quarters and partners. After the boys had selected their tents, the male teachers moved into those tents where they thought there might be a problem. On both camping trips, there was only one accompanying female teacher. On the trip with the girls, she chose a centrally located tent to sleep in. The men slept at the summer troop house which was in earshot of the tents in the event of an emergency.

After arriving and setting up, the students had a sack lunch that they had brought from home. After lunch the groups were divided for classes. The boys were in six groups of about five each, and the girls had five groups of about nine each.

The following represents the girls' schedule which was slightly refined from that of the boys, in that fewer classes were planned for longer time periods. This schedule seemed to work best for both students and staff.

	Thursday
9:00	leave school
10:30	arrive at camp
10:30 - 12:30	set up and have lunch
12:30 - 5:00	three 90-minute classes
5:00 - 6:30	supper and log writing
6:30 - 8:00	visit pig farm
8:00	campfire and snack
11:00	bed
	Friday
6:00	arise, shower, and pack
7:00 - 9:00	breakfast
9:00 - 12:00	two 90-minute classes
12:00 - 1:30	lunch
1:30 - 3:00	final class
3:00 - 5:00	clean-up, tug of war, snack
5:00	leave for home
7:00	arrive at school

A neighboring farmer invited both groups of students to visit his pig farm. The students hiked two miles in the evening to his farm and were able to hand feed his pigs, as well as see his beef cattle and ponies.

All students shared in the cooking of the three meals over an open fire. First, they gathered enough firewood for the meals. They used matches to get the fire going. Each student was assigned a task to do to prepare the meal. After the cooking and eating, there was a clean-up which also involved everyone. Each student had been asked to bring a "dip bag" (an old nylon stocking or wash cloth sewn together) to wash their dishes. There were three pails of water for washing dishes after each meal. The first one was warm water with soap for a wash. The second was rinse with hot water, and the third was another rinse with hot water and several drops of bleach for sanitizing. The dip bags were used for both rinses. The large pots also had to be cleaned in this manner. When finished, the dip bags were hung from a tree so the dishes could dry and be ready for the next meal.

Before leaving camp on Tuesday, the first group performed a general clean-up of the area. The supplies for each class were stored and food which could be saved for the next group was refrigerated. When the second group left camp on Friday, everything had to be spotless before the camp caretakers would check the students out. Everyone was given clean-up chores (buildings, grounds, food packing, etc.) with the teachers supervising the packing of their own supplies and the van and camper.

Equipment List for Camp

In addition to what you wear to camp, you will need the following:

Sleeping bag or bedroll	toothbrush
raincoat or poncho	tooth paste
boots	comb
1 pair sturdy shoes	deodorant (stick-no spray)
2 clean shirts	handkerchief
1 clean pair pants or jeans	plastic bowl
clean change of underwear	plastic cup
2 pair clean socks	spoon
sweater or sweatshirt	2 pens
jacket	2 pencils
hat	notebook
wash cloth	work gloves (if you have)
small towel	dip bag (old nylon stocking, clean)
bar of soap	envelope with stamp on it

These things may not be brought under any circumstances:

gym shoes	hair curlers
suitcase	anything electric or battery operated
flashlight	radio
pillow	shampoo
purse	knife
make-up	drugs
jewelry	cigarettes
candy or gum	fireworks

Faculty must be notified of all medications brought to camp.

PROGRAM ACTIVITIES

Camp activities were planned by each of the six participating teachers. The following are the activities, listed by discipline, that were carried out by both the boys and the girls during each two-day trip.

Physical Education: Students travelled the length of the creek leading to the Fox River. They crawled, ran, jumped, climbed, and walked over, under, or through all objects in their path. They were instructed to leave nature as they found it. This was a "follow the leader" activity with the instructor leading the way. When the students reached the river, a "stone skipping" contest was held. The second day's P.E. was devoted to climbing a large tree and traveling across a suspended rope hanging from one tree to another. This proved to be the most daring camp activity and the most talked about adventure of the trip. A steep "hill climb" race was held with each contestant racing against a stop watch.

Science: The assistant principal conducted a class on plants. He wanted the students to recognize common plants and know their characteristics; to learn about the uses, peculiar qualities, and interesting aspects of different plants; and to understand some of the interrelationships of plant and animal life. To accomplish this, he took students on a nature hike and identified different types of environments (forest, swamp, river bed, cultivated, sandy, rocky, etc.), and the life forms occupying each ecosystem. He and the students located edible fruit bearing plants in the area, looked at evidence of animal and insect habitats (ants, squirrels, birds, deer, insects, snakes, etc.), and examined examples of plant and insect effects on decomposition of plants.

Another science teacher exposed students to various aspects of stream ecology. The students observed and collected specimens to be cataloged. Two stages of the stream, mature and old age, were investigated to discover the relationship of plant and animal communities to the topography of the ecosystem. Students used microscopes, slides, test tubes, hand lenses, minnow traps, lugol's solution, taxonomic keys, dip nets, forceps, and needles in their stream study.

A third science class was concerned with creating a woodland terrarium. Materials included a gallon jar, woodland soil and plants, and collecting tools. To begin, each group held a discussion about the interdependence of plants and animals in the environment. Students were taken on a short walk to collect typical woodland plants such as mosses, ferns, pine seedlings, fungi, wild strawberries, violets, etc. While on the hike, the teacher pointed out poison ivy and discussed its similarity to Virginia Creeper. Upon returning to the troophouse, the students built individual terrariums which were later displayed at the school.

Social Studies: The social studies teacher worked with students on pace, direction, the compass, mapping, measuring, and estimating. In order to measure the height of a tree and the width of the river, students had to find their pace for three meters. Students also found direction using the shadow of the sun and a watch. Students next learned how to use the compass, reading direction as well as degrees. After mastering these skills, the students made a map of the area.

Language Arts: The pupils kept a log of their activities, wrote a letter home, and listed descriptive words to define natural surroundings. They also discussed the meanings of some old sayings, went over some plant and animal identification charts, took notes, wrote and followed directions, worked on figures of speech, and studied modifying words. The students also wrote Haiku poetry.

Art and Music: Although there was not a specific art class, art projects were included in other classes. Some of these projects were sand casting, leaf prints, spatter prints, finger painting, and nature drawings. Music in the form of group singing occurred around the campfire in the evening.

Sample Activity
by Bob Facklam

How to Estimate Heights Using the Shadow-Ratio Method

Procedure:

1. Place stick of known length (yardstick or meterstick recommended) perpendicular to the ground and measure the length of shadow.
2. Measure shadow cast by object to be measured (tree).

Solve this proportion:

Shadow of Object—Object's Height
Shadow of Stick—Stick's Height

Example: 3 ft. yardstick casts 2 ft. shadow
Tree casts 10 ft. shadow

$$\frac{10}{2} = \frac{\text{Tree's Height}}{3}$$

Tree's Height = 15 ft.

STUDENT EVALUATION

A questionnaire was given to each student who had attended the field trip. The following are some of the questions and results from the survey.

1. In past years, the eighth-grade field trip has consisted of a trip to Springfield, a tour of Chicago, or something comparable. Did you prefer the outdoor educational trip or would you have preferred the usual trip? Why? Every student responded that he preferred the outdoor trip and some of the reasons given were: "... because it was outdoors; was not the regular class; met people on a different level (especially the teachers); enjoyed the team work; and had never done this before."

2. Had you ever camped like this before? If so, when and how many times? Sixty-three percent of the students had done some camping. Of these, the number of times ranged from one to a high of fifteen. The average number of times seemed to be about three.

3. Please list the new experiences you had at the camp. Those listed included the following: "measuring the height of a tree; measuring the width of a river; finding direction from a watch; making a campfire; learning the different types of trees; visiting a pig farm; using a compass; sleeping in a platform tent; climbing a rope over the river; building a terrarium; walking in the creek or river; climbing trees; seeing a different side of the teachers; cleaning the latrines; cooking around a campfire; writing a Haiku; sleeping outdoors; skipping stones; drinking well water; cooking over an open fire; seeing and touching a stinging nettle bush; learning about poison ivy; building a fire; and learning what ecology and conservation are about."

4. Which classes did you enjoy most? Why? The students seemed to like the classes in which they were physically challenged; that is, physical education, social studies, and science classes. Their comments were: "It was daring; we were like the explorers; enjoyed the climbing; it was rugged." Many liked the language arts class because it was: "peaceful, relaxing, and restful." A large number of students said that they enjoyed every class because all were different and learning was made fun. "We didn't even know we were learning something!"

5. Had you ever been to a pig farm before? Please list new sights or learning experiences. Of those responding, 67% had never been to a pig farm before. Some of the new experiences listed were: "touching a pig; the smell of the farm; touching the electric fence; and seeing a real white horse."

6. What did you enjoy most about the trip? The large number responded that they enjoyed the hikes the most. Others listed in order of preference: "the campfire at night; everything; cooking; sleeping in tents; classes; rope climbing; team work; farm; and terrarium."

7. What did you enjoy least about the trip? Students listed the following: "nothing; the ride home; the horn in the morning to get us up; classes; going home; breakfast; bugs and mosquitos; getting up at 6 am; cooking; and going to bed early."

8. If we had time to go again, would you go? Why or why not? The results were 100% "yes!" The reason given by most of the students was "because it was fun." The next highest reason was "because it was educational." Others listed: "because it was outdoors; out of the city; out of school, and peaceful." One student responded that this trip had created a desire to join the backpacking and wilderness club in high school.

9. Do you think next year's eighth-grade class should take the same trip? Overwhelmingly the students said, "yes!"

10. Is there any way the trip could have been improved? Of those replying, 54%

said "no." Others listed the following: "allow flashlights; more free time; stay longer; better syrup at breakfast; not so many classes; and more sleep time."

The last section of the questionnaire was for additional comments. Some students had suggestions for things the staff might do to improve the program and others used the space to compliment the trip. The remarks included, "I wish we could have gone swimming. It should have been longer. Let's do it again! The trip was a blast! It was really nice of the teachers to take their time with us. There seemed to always be something new to learn. I enjoyed it. It was fun!"

STAFF RECOMMENDATIONS

The six teachers attending the camp came up with some recommendations of their own for future trips.

These included the following: Do not try to take both groups to the camp within the same week. Take one group on a Thursday and Friday and then take the second group on the following Thursday and Friday. (The staff was exhausted after two trips in one week!) Keep the classes small with a ratio of no more than ten students to one teacher. Another suggestion was that the school district should hire some substitutes to cover the classes that stay behind. The classes were too large for those teachers who did not go on the trip.

Finally, if the camping program is continued, the staff would like to go twice—once in the fall of the year and once again in the spring, so that the students could see the major differences that occur over the winter months.

All in all, the trip was a great success and a rewarding experience for both students and staff.

BIBLIOGRAPHY

Discovering Nature: 135 Nature Activities, Educational Insights, Inc., Inglewood, California, 1971.

Donaldson, George and Oswald Goering, Perspectives on Outdoor Education Readings, William C. Brown Company, Dubuque, Iowa, 1974.

Hammerman, Donald R. and William M. Hammerman, Teaching in the Outdoors, Burgess Publications, Minneapolis, Minnesota, 1973.

Madison, John P., John A. Glanzer, Matthew J. Ludes, and Lonie Rudd, "Stations Outdoors," Science and Children, p. 15-16, November, 1976.

Needham, James G. and Paul R. Needham, A Guide to the Study of Fresh-Water Biology, Holden-Day, San Francisco, California, April, 1973.

Nickelsburg, Janet, Field Trips: Ecology for Youth Leaders, Burgess Publications, Minneapolis, Minnesota, 1966.

Creative Learning Environments for the Middle School

Robert S. Jones
C. Kenneth McEwin

Built environments for children are usually designed by adults, for adult use and for adult convenience. Consequently, such environments may not meet the needs of the children who inhabit them. This has been particularly true of schools used by children in the transescent stage, which begins prior to the onset of puberty and extends through the early stages of adolescence.

The transition from the primary classroom to the middle school almost always requires a major psychological adjustment for children. Yet school designs seldom serve to support the child during this transition. It would appear that educators plan activities and design curricula independent of their environmental setting.

Indoor space designs for transescents are patterned after those provided for high school students. Consequently, they fail to fit the behavior patterns of transescents. They tend to ignore psychological needs for small spaces that accommodate independent study, learning and social interaction, as well as the need for solitude during quiet time.

The transescent, no less than the young child, needs adequate space for movement and exploration. Classroom designs that require pupils to remain seated for long periods of time are unrealistic in terms of what we know about early adolescent growth and development.

Transescents have need to touch, explore and manipulate, to become intimately involved in encounter with their environment. Too often educators proceed as though all middle school youngsters have reached a formal stage of intellectual development characterized solely by abstract reasoning. On the contrary, abundant data support a primary need for hands-on activities that facilitate the learning process. An excellent starting point, and perhaps a major safeguard for designers of middle school learning spaces, is to create environments responsive to human needs. A responsive environment allows children (1) to explore freely, (2) to be aware of the consequences of their behavior, and (3) to learn at their own rates.

* * *

A necessary starting point in planning middle school learning environments is concern for the ways in which transescents learn. The following suggest ways in which environments may respond to learning styles:

Transescents learn through doing. Provide ample space for movement involved in exploration, manipulation and experimentation; provide space for activities related to hobbies and interest groups.
Transescents learn through conversing and interacting with peers. Plan space design that allows for places to accommodate small groups.

Transescents learn through reading. Provide carefully designed reading areas with a variety of reading materials in such a way that each classroom has its own "mini-library."

Transescents learn through seeing and listening. Provide a media center, study carrel, listening center with earphones and small projection rooms.

Transescents learn through role-playing and fantasy. Include space in school design for dramatic activities that provide opportunities for trying out for roles, for gaining insights into the behaviors of others, and for exploring feelings. In a major sense, such space helps to create a psychological environment that allows for healthy personality development.

Transescents learn through independent thinking and investigation. Provide quiet areas and small spaces for individual study—an important mode of learning.

Transescents learn through exploring natural and created environments. Expand classroom walls to include the world outside, thus extending the transescents' world and enabling greater understanding of ecological and sociological concerns.

Transescents learn through vigorous body movement. Provide large spaces, indoors and outdoors, for movement and release of substantial amounts of energy.

Transescents vary greatly in development, needs and learning styles. Plan learning environments that are flexible enough to respond to individual differences.

CHECKLIST FOR TEACHERS

Given the particular psychological and behavorial needs of transescents and the wide variety of learning styles identified here, there is a need for some systematic evaluation of school environments. To be effective, the learning climate must be based on the characteristics of the students who inhabit them. The following checklist may serve as a useful and simple means by which teachers can determine how well their own classrooms rate as a good place for learning.

Environmental Feature	Good	Average	Poor	No Provisions
1. Ample space for movement	_____	_____	_____	_____
2. Areas for exploration	_____	_____	_____	_____
3. Wide variety of easily accessible materials	_____	_____	_____	_____
4. Activity areas for hobbies and interest groups	_____	_____	_____	_____
5. Activity areas easily defined	_____	_____	_____	_____
6. Bulletin boards and work displayed	_____	_____	_____	_____
7. Places for small groups	_____	_____	_____	_____

8. Mini-library	_____	_____	_____	_____
9. Reading areas	_____	_____	_____	_____
10. Private carrels or listening center	_____	_____	_____	_____
11. Media center	_____	_____	_____	_____
12. Areas for drama and role play	_____	_____	_____	_____
13. Quiet areas	_____	_____	_____	_____
14. Availability and access to outside areas	_____	_____	_____	_____
15. Large spaces for vigorous body movement, both indoors and outdoors	_____	_____	_____	_____
16. Environmental flexibility	_____	_____	_____	_____

CONCLUSION

Although the checklist above focuses on physical features of the environment, a number of other factors associated with the learning climate are equally significant. Without them even the best physical facility will fail to provide an appropriate climate for learning. Donald Eichhorn* suggests some that seem essential. The environment must be: (1) learner-centered, (2) creative, (3) industrious, (4) flexible, (5) dynamic, (6) friendly, (7) exploratory, (8) loving/caring and (9) disciplined.

The need for focusing more closely on learning environments in middle schools is apparent as we move toward realizing the most ideal places in which to educate transescent youngsters. School planners and administrators, linked in their thinking to traditional and conservative ideas of school classrooms, must now take the leadership in designing environments that most accurately respond to our present knowledge of the behavioral needs and learning styles of transescents. Any delay in narrowing the gap between knowledge and practice does serious injustice to children and to those who have sought to create exciting and rewarding middle schools.

Very few plants thrive in infertile soil. Very few middle school students will reach their full potential in rigid, noncreative learning environments. It is hoped that the brief, and certainly limited, ideas presented here will (1) raise the level of awareness among those responsible for the development of middle school education and (2) stimulate widespread interest in investigating further the learning needs of transescents and the environments provided for them.

---

*Eichhorn, Donald H. "The Power of an Idea," *Journal of the North Carolina League of Middle/Junior High Schools*, 1979.

Self-Assessment of Your Middle/Junior High Science Program*

The purpose of this instrument is to assist you and other members of your department to obtain general information about the strong aspects and the areas in need of improvement in your middle/junior high science program. Information from the data should assist you in making long-range plans for program improvement and identifying possible solutions to problem areas.

In completing the assessment, you will need to duplicate the matrix grid so it may be used to rate each statement. The grid has been reproduced here only once in order to conserve space.

Rate each of the following statements on the matrix according to the two parameters: Desirability for your school and then Achievement in your school. Each statement should first be evaluated for its Desirability. The scales used for each are:

Desirability
- 4—very desirable
- 3—desirable
- 2—moderately desirable
- 1—unimportant
- -1—undesirable

Achievement
- 4—excellent
- 3—very good
- 2—moderate
- 1—low
- -1—avoided

- The major purpose of science education in our school is to lay the foundation for students to take more science.
- The science program in our school undergoes major change or modification every five years.
- Science courses reveal a variety of career opportunities, regardless of sex or ethnic background, in science and other related occupations.
- Science provides opportunities for students to have experiences similar to those of practicing scientists, i.e., to identify problems, use the library, design methods for the study of problems, carry through projects using equipment and write reports.
- The skills learned in mathematics are useful in solving problems in science courses.

---

*Adapted from the National Science Teachers Association publication *Guidelines for Self-Assessment of Secondary School Science Programs*. The complete five part "Guidelines" is available for $10 from NSTA Special Publications, 1742 Connecticut Avenue, NW, Washington, DC 20009.

- Our science teachers know what they are doing and why; they have goals and plans for their courses; they come to each class meeting well prepared.
- Our science teachers realize that science study has different appeals and values for different students. They do not "turn-off" everyone not planning to become a scientist or engineer.
- Science courses have helped to improve the students' basic skills (reading, writing, mathematics).
- Our teachers encourage students to make suggestions for strengthening the science program and improving instruction. They evaluate the suggestions and make an effort to use them.
- Our school guidance counselors know a lot about science-related careers and the school science program. They give helpful advice in the selection of science courses.
- The science courses offered in our school include the requirements for every student to spend at least 20 percent of the total class time in individual or small group laboratory investigations.
- Our science program extends science study beyond the school into the nearby community or beyond (e.g., field trips, visits to industry, camping experiences).
- The science courses tend to be abstract and theoretical rather than applied or practical.
- Literature assigned in English courses includes topics about science and/or technology.
- Science teachers show genuine, personalized interest in the students.
- The effects of science and technology on our society are dealt with in social studies courses.
- The science program development in our school is influenced by the continuous evaluation of the science curriculum.
- The most intense pressure for science program change or modification comes from the central administration of our school district.
- Science courses should prepare individuals to utilize science for improving their own lives and coping with an increasingly technological world.
- The science program provides students an opportunity to study the effects of technological developments on society.
- Science courses provide an opportunity for students to apply their knowledge and skills to attempt to solve real problems in the community.
- The science program includes topics of current events, future problems, issues, and needs confronting society.
- The content and nature of specific science courses are influenced by national curriculum development projects carried on during the past fifteen years or so.
- Science includes discussions of abuses of science and technology by humans.
- The science program development for our school includes consideration of recommendations from a K-12 curriculum committee for our school district or from the other elementary or secondary schools attended by our students.

- The science program development includes consideration of ideas, suggestions, and criticisms solicited from interested, concerned persons other than the staff and administration; e.g., current and former students, parents, prospective employers, and others.
- Science program development includes provision by the school district for specialists, expert leadership and/or counsel to assist staff and curriculum committees with their work.
- Preparatory steps are taken prior to general adoption of courses or innovations; e.g., pilot testing and evaluation; inservice programs for teachers; explanation of proposals to students, parents, and concerned citizens.
- Our science teachers are knowledgeable about the total science program of the district and the various student activities completed at each grade.
- The Board of Education of our district is aware of the current status of the science program and future needs.
- Our science program includes multidisciplinary aspects through joint planning with other curriculum areas such as English, social studies, mathematics, industrial arts.
- Science program development has resulted from curriculum work accomplished during school vacation time or release time.
- The majority of science teachers have attended within the past three years at least one meeting, convention, or conference held by a national, state or citywide science education organization.
- A formal evaluation of the science program has been conducted within the past seven years by an outside science consultant such as from a college, state education department, or county board of education.

- Science enrollment statistics are gathered and examined to determine whether any identifiable groups of students are not well served by the program, e.g., low achievers, minority students, females, students for whom English is a second language.
- In evaluating a student's progress, care is taken to minimize the effect of such factors as cultural bias of instruments (and teachers), reading difficulties, and physical handicaps.
- Students are involved in evaluation of curriculum, courses, and activities.
- Each science course evaluates the psychomotor skills developed in the laboratory portion by means of a practicum.
- The science staff has visited other schools to establish standards of comparison.
- Almost all of the science class time is involved in teacher lectures, question-answers, and textbook readings.
- Almost all laboratory activities are conducted as teacher demonstrations.
- Our science facilities include classroom and laboratory activity areas which adapt well for each course that is taught.
- Our classrooms and laboratory areas are adequate in number and size for the number of students who take science courses.

- The size of individual laboratory work surfaces is adequate; i.e., approximately one square meter per student.
- Each classroom area includes a demonstration table provided with essential services and located so that demonstrations can be viewed by the entire class.
- An outdoor nature study area is available on or near the school grounds or campus.
- Storage areas are adjacent or readily accessible to the classrooms or laboratories where the materials are used.
- Special storage facilities and security measures are provided for items and materials that are particularly costly, delicate, or that are hazardous, poisonous, or flammable.
- Evaluation of teacher performance is followed up through discussion of observations and other data, culminating in recommendations for professional growth activities to improve performance.
- Released time and substitutes are provided in support of teachers who participate as officers, as committee members, and in the meetings of science teacher organizations.
- In our total science department, at least one person has been designated chairman with an adjusted teaching load to provide at least 20 percent of the school work week for administrative and supervisory duties.
- The allocation of funds for the science department budget recognizes that a threshold amount is needed to support any science course, as well as a per student allocation.
- When items are cut from the science budget, the teachers determine what is to be cut.
- The science department has a priority list of capital outlay equipment which should be obtained during the next few years.

Activities

Science teaching may have become astronomy without the stars . . . botany without the flowers . . . geology without the mountains and valleys.

Frank Press, President
National Academy of Sciences

Content should be relevant to the students' lives and should be material that can be organized into meaningful and participatory learning experiences appropriate to the developmental level of these students.

Paul DeHart Hurd, et al.
*The Status of Middle School and
Junior High School Science*

. . . learning has to be an active process, because knowledge is a construction from within.

Constance Kamii
Piaget in the Classroom

The Rockshop

David J. Quattropani

Students at King Philip Junior High School have a rockshop as an alternative to the traditional study hall and science club. The rockshop gives them a chance to take part in a creative endeavor while learning. Rock tumbling, making of cabochons, faceting, and making finished jewelry are part of the daily activity.

This program evolved partly because many students do not make full use of their time in traditional study halls; also, science is often seen by this age group as a subject fit only for the laboratory, having little relation to other areas. The rockshop has helped eliminate this attitude. There were parts of two rock tumblers and a lapidary machine in our science department, collecting dust and serving no purpose. A cooperative principal, a teacher with high interest and motivation, and high student interest led to the concept of the rockshop.

First, helped by interested students, we assembled the rock tumblers, set up a water supply, and started tumbling the first stones. After the first batch of stones was polished we saw student reactions to the beauty of the stones and began to realize the potential for stimulating interest in geology. Students could see the similarity between rock tumbling (an artificial process using grits) and weathering (a natural process). They could learn that some stones, because of hardness, take longer to tumble than other, softer stones. While students were selecting stones to work with, they could learn about mineral content. Furthermore, they learned they could create art forms from common rocks. Soon the rockshop became popular and we required more equipment and supplies.

Soon we bought a diamond saw. With the help of a local technical school, we set up the lapidary machine that could be used for grinding, sanding, and polishing. The process could now be expanded from mere rock tumbling to cutting and shaping slab stone. When we set the shaped stones into jewelry settings, enthusiasm and interest blossomed among the students. We applied to the administration for a mini-grant to spend on a program with the following objectives:

1. To have students appreciate the art and science of jewelry making.
2. To foster a relationship between the art, industrial arts, and science departments.
3. To provide students with an alternative to study hall.
4. To let students become acquainted with the basic concepts of geology.
5. To foster an appreciation for jewelry making as both an art form and a way of creative self-expression.
6. To allow and encourage students to pursue and complete their own projects.
7. To have students work in a one-to-one relationship with a teacher or with other students.

The mini-grant money allowed us to buy lights, a faceting machine, two more lapidary machines, and a grinding arbor. Our equipment was supplied without motors; we visited washing machine repair shops to obtain free or inexpensive

Art by Lydia Nolan-Davis

motors. Students, teachers, and others helped to get the new machines operable and safe for use. Soon, we had a well-equipped and functional rockshop.

When the shop came into full operation, students learned about the geology of rocks, how to create beautiful jewelry, how to run and care for machinery, and how to instruct new rockshop participants in the various stages of the jewelry making process. Our objectives were being met. The school also has special classes for students with learning disabilities. Some of these students have become involved in the rockshop program. All students have experienced success and enjoyment.

Success of programs often generates new problems. The rockshop is becoming expensive. Science department funds can buy grits, sanding discs, and grinding wheels, considered maintenance items; but jewelry settings and good slab stone, which become student property, are expensive. We are currently considering a new phase in our program which may solve our financial problems as well as provide students some career and life education. In this phase, students who participate in the rockshop program will elect officers and a board of directors. This group may issue stock in our rockshop company. Local merchants, parents, and students not in the program have expressed interest in buying our jewelry. A certain percentage of our production may be sold to generate funds so we can declare dividends and reinvest funds into needed supplies. If business is good our stock value might even go up!

Besides relieving our economic concerns, this new aspect of our program will expose students to the world of finance, the laws of economics, and the functioning of a company.

Archeology In the Classroom

Lois M. J. Danes

Last year was the first year of the Danes School Archeology Project (DSAP). The project offered grades six through nine a hands-on situation involving scientific investigating, reasoning, and problem solving. The intent was to devote time daily for one month to acquiring the basic skills of archeologists on a dig.

New Bern, the original capital of North Carolina, and its surrounding area hold much history that remains uninvestigated. A local landowner permitted us to dig on her property in search of historical remains.

Forty students would work on the site one and a half hours a day for a month. The size of the site was defined by the staff; within the larger site, however, students marked off several 3 × 4 meter (m) sites. Students worked in teams of two throughout the dig.

The first day of the program was spent in the classroom, familiarizing students with the project and equipment, identifying each team's responsibilities, and making sure the students knew the steps required in an investigation of this type. Students were cautioned not to scavenge. Isolated artifacts are not helpful when seeking historical information about an area.

Our first trip to the site revealed problems. Tree roots, rocks, and wash gullies prevented digging in parts of the designated area. Despite this, each team chose a site, and, working around obstacles when necessary, plotted out a rectangle. No site was less than 3-m long or 2-m wide.

Once the area was plotted, each team drove stakes into the ground to mark the corners of the site, and strung heavy twine at ground level to define the area and guide digging.

Next, four screening tables were built. The tables measured 1 m × 1 m × 75 cm and were built out of pine. Fine mesh screening 1 m × 1 m covered the bottom. The tables were used to sift dirt in search of artifacts.

The dig proceeded. Each team had its own artifact bag, metric ruler, pencil, kneeling pads, and gloves.

Digging to 15-cm depths, the students soon learned to scrape with the edge of the trowel to create a smooth table with perpendicular sides. The depth at which artifacts were found helped us determine their age and the conditions surrounding their deposit. One member of each team troweled, while the other scooped out loosened soil (grubbings) for screening at the table.

UNCOVERING ARTIFACTS

Eventually, the students found a few bones and other artifacts. In classroom sessions, students examined items found on the site, cleaning the finds and identifying them as bone or non-bone. If the item was a bone, what made it distinguishable as such and from what type of animal did it come? If not a bone, what was it? (See chart.)

Bone Chart

Bones in different parts of a body have different shapes and sizes. To get some idea of where a bone is from, look at its shape. Here are a few general rules:

Bones of feet and hands tend to look like shortened copies of long bones. Small, dense bones with many sides may be from the wrist or ankle.

Bones of arms (or wings) and legs tend to be long and slender with knobs or depressions on the ends. They are called long bones.

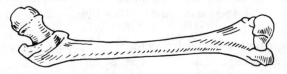

Flat bones usually come from the head (cranium), hip (pelvis, innominate) or shoulder blade (scapula). In large animals, rib pieces may be broad and flat. Bones from a skull (cranium) may have jagged edges called sutures where two bones come together. They may have branching grooves on the inside for blood vessels.

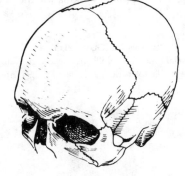

Vertebrae are complex, many sided bones with flat, knobby and/or spiny portions. Vertebrae from different types of animals differ in appearance.

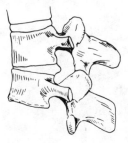

Art by Robyn Johnson-Ross

We developed hypotheses regarding the artifacts. Some of the hypotheses were verified by talking with the property owner; many had to be left unanswered pending further research.

In one of the dig's most exciting moments, the students uncovered charred bits of wood buried in the second and third layers. We hypothesized (and verified) that the area had once suffered a minor fire.

In two of the plots outstanding soil changes had occurred. Soil texture and color differed from other areas. Students theorized that animal burrows had caved in, or holes had developed due to rain run-off and had filled with sediment. Neither theory could be verified.

In addition to bones and bits of wood, the students unearthed pot shards of the Early Woodland Indian period and pieces of 18th, 19th, and 20th Century china and pottery.

At the close of the sessions, students wrote articles about their experience for the school paper, and asked that the dig be repeated next year.

Hearing about our school project, the local historical society asked some of our students to participate in a special dig at a local homesite. Six students who had demonstrated skill and understanding of archeological techniques volunteered and spent mornings for one week assisting a state archeologist with the project.

The value of the opportunity for students to experience a dig, work with a professional archeologist, and apply new skills for the benefit of the community cannot be over-emphasized.

BIBLIOGRAPHY
1. *Zooarcheological Field Guide*. Foundation of Illinois Archeology, Kampsville, IL. 1976.
2. Gallant, Roy. "Who Were the First Americans?" *Science 81*, 2:94; April 1981.

Classroom Planetarium

Paul Ankney

Teaching star constellations and planetary motion is not easy, particularly because stars are not visible during normal school hours. While star patterns may be drawn on the chalkboard, projected on a screen or on the ceiling, or pictured in photographs, most children have difficulty applying what they see in the classroom to the night sky.

Why do students find it difficult to transfer classroom instruction in astronomy to the night sky? Children are generally unable to deal with:
- Higher abstractions such as dots on a chalkboard, which represent stars in a symbolic way only;
- Large differences in scale (the contrast between the sizes of star patterns on a star map and their sizes in the night sky is immense);
- Orientation (many children have difficulty with compass directions in the daytime, let alone at night).

These difficulties are compounded by the Earth's rotation, which makes stars appear to rise and set, by gradually changing orientations of the constellations from hour to hour, by the Earth's annual revolution around the sun, and by our planet's 23½° axial tilt. The latter two factors produce a slowly changing set of stars from month to month. In addition, the planets move across the sky at different rates, and even seem, at times, to move backward; both phenomena are generally incomprehensible prior to high school or college physics.

Thus, children and even some adults might seem incapable of learning much about planetary motion and the night sky. Certain sky constellations, however, can be learned easily, and students can use these as reference points for further learning.

THREE-DIMENSIONAL MODEL

With assistance from the teacher, students can build a low-cost, three-dimensional model of the night sky which can help them understand constellations. The model is a lightweight dome that hangs from the ceiling. Papier-mache and chicken wire mesh make a fine dome but substitute materials are possible. The dome need not be exactly hemispherical, since our view of the night sky seldom extends all the way down to the horizon in all directions. Any arching shape will suggest the three dimensionality of the sky, but the larger the dome's diameter, the better.

Figure 1 illustrates a suitable shape for a classroom night-sky model, or planetarium. After the model is constructed and hung overhead, place compass direction markers around the rim, with north on the same side of the model as actual north in the environment. The most prominent star group in the Northern Hemisphere, the Big Dipper,* is then marked on the interior surface of the dome with reasonable

---

*The Big Dipper is not itself a constellation, but forms part of the constellation Ursa Major. The Little Dipper forms almost the entirety of Ursa Minor.

accuracy of size and shape. Orient the Dipper as it would appear at 8:00 p.m. during the current month. A planisphere (such as Philips') and a star map (available in good bookstores, many astronomy books, and *Science and Children*'s monthly Sky Calendar) assist greatly in this. Next, glue white beads or other small round objects onto the dome to represent stars. Larger stars can be represented by larger beads, and so on, so that the beads correspond to each star's apparent magnitude.

OBSERVING THE SKY

After each child has had an unhurried opportunity to stand or sit under the model and review what is overhead, the class should look for the Big Dipper in the night sky. An 8:00 p.m. viewing time will match the 8:00 p.m. positions of the stars on the classroom model, making it easy for students to relate the night sky to the model.

Once children know the Big Dipper and its sister star group, the Little Dipper, they can add nearby star groups to the model. For realism, the students might use beads of different colors for stars of different colors—pale blue for Rigel and Sirius, red for Betelgeuse, yellow for Capella, etc. Suggest another 8:00 p.m. stargaze, so students can again compare what they see in the heavens to the model. As the weeks go by, add constellations to the model one at a time, moving outward in arcs from the Big and Little Dippers. Students can continue checking the model against the night sky until they feel satisfied with their knowledge of the sky. The visible planets should also be placed on the model in their present positions. The students need not learn every constellation, since the major objectives of such instruction are to help children learn to appreciate the pleasures of knowledgeably observing the stars, of being able to orient themselves at night, and of comprehending to some extent the motions of planetary bodies.

REFERENCES
1. Zim, Herbert S., and Robert H. Baker. *Stars*. Golden Press, New York, NY. 1975.
2. Mayall, R. Newton, Margaret Mayall and Jerome Wyckoff. *The Sky Observer's Guide*. Golden Press, New York, NY. 1971.
3. Victor, Robert C. "Spectacular Triple Conjunction." *Science and Children*, 18:3, November/December 1980.
4. Gallant, Roy A. *The Constellations: How They Came To Be*, Four Winds Press, New York, NY. 1979.

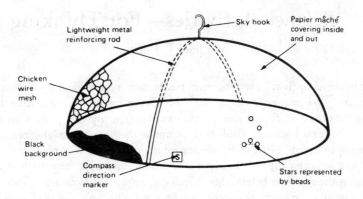

Figure 1
How To Construct the Dome

1. Form a circle that will be the rim around the bottom of the dome. (Suggested diameter is 0.9 to 1.8 meters.) Bend one or more rods into curved pieces to form the rim. Fasten the ends of the rods together by binding the overlapped ends with a strong yet flexible wire. Use pliers to tighten the wire securely. Bend any sharp ends over.
2. Form arches by bending metal rod into curved pieces. Attach each arch by binding the ends of the arch to the rim with wire. (Three arches should provide a good framework for the chicken wire mesh.)
3. Wrap wire around the arches where they cross at the top of the dome. Tighten the wire securely.
4. Using a coathanger or other stiff wire, form and attach a hook (or loop) at the top of the dome.
5. Hang the dome framework at a convenient working height. Cover it with chicken wire mesh. Bind the mesh to the arches and rim with wire.
6. Papier-mache the outside of the dome. When it is dry, take down the dome, turn it over, and papier-mache the inside.
7. Paint the inside of the dome black with Tempera or other paint. Several coats may be necessary.
8. Rehang the dome at working height and paint the outside (your choice of colors).
9. Hang the dome high enough to stand under for viewing but low enough so that the children can attach beads (representing stars) while standing on a stool.
10. Using a compass, glue direction markers on east, south, west, and north locations around the rim.
11. Consult a star map to determine the proper orientation of the Big Dipper for the current month. Hold the star map over your head with north corresponding to the north marker on the rim of the dome. Mark the stars of the Big Dipper on the inside of the dome. Glue beads onto the dome at these locations. (Locate the Big Dipper very carefully. It is the reference point for all other star groups to be added later.)

Science Activities—For Thinking

Michael J. Padilla

The word "activity" over the years has become synonymous with those things that are good in science education. New science teachers leave teacher training programs ready to change the system, to call on the mystical powers involved in activity oriented science. Publishers promote their textbooks and programs as "activity centered," often with little regard to actual content. Professional journals support activities through first person success stories and how-to-do-it articles. What is the rationale behind this "hands-on" approach? Why are activities considered more appropriate than other methods for achieving science objectives? Just what is an activity? Is it possible that certain kinds of activities might contribute more to learning science in the middle school than others? These questions are the major focus of this article. After discussing several salient arguments for inclusion of activities in the curriculum, different kinds of activities will be defined and one special type—process skill activities—will be analyzed and illustrated.

WHY SHOULD ACTIVITIES BE ADVOCATED FOR MIDDLE SCHOOL AGED STUDENTS?

Doing and Understanding

One of the most common justifications for promoting activities in science classrooms is embodied in the axiom:

> I hear . . . and I forget
> I see . . . and I remember
> I do . . . and I understand
>
> Ancient Chinese Proverb quoted from
> *The ESS Reader*
> (Elementary Science Study, 1970).

The implication of this saying is that the learner will better understand and retain knowledge when first-hand, manipulative experience is possible. This seems quite reasonable especially when an activity is performed in the proper context of a unit. That is, activities appropriately connected to previous and future work can enhance knowledge acquisition.

Development

Science educators have long used developmental arguments for utilizing science activities. With the increased popularity of Piagetian theory, the view that children learn through activity which allows them to discover, internalize, and build their own understandings and meanings has emerged. Piaget states "It is absolutely necessary that learners have at their disposal concrete material experiences (and not merely pictures), and that they form their own hypotheses and verify them (or not verify them) themselves through their own active manipulations" (in Schwebel and Raph, 1973, pp. IX-X).

Recent findings relative to the onset and development of formal operational abilities tend to reinforce the need for an activity oriented curriculum. Evidence (Lovell, 1961; Chiapetta, 1976) indicates that most early adolescents have not begun to develop formal abilities at age 11-12 as Piaget originally hypothesized. Renner, et al., (1978) found only 17% of 7th graders and 25% of 8th graders operating at a formal level. Piaget (1972) reassessed his earlier work and hypothesized that his orignial subjects may have been a privileged group that displayed accelerated abilities. Whatever the reason the fact that few middle school children exhibit formal abilities indicates a very strong need for using an activity approach in the middle school.

Nature of the Transescent

The very nature of the transescent supports a strong argument for activities in the middle school. Physical growth during these years is highly irregular. Muscular and body framework development often take place disproportionately, resulting in awkwardness and self consciousness. Increased physical activity is often a product of the typical high energy level of children this age. Thus the physical aspects of moving and manipulation during an activity fit their developmental needs. Similar changes are occurring emotionally, with individuals simultaneously manifesting both adult and child-like behaviors. Self assertion and independence are regularly mixed with insecurity and instability (Georgiady and Romano, 1977). Activities can provide an important outlet for these energies and feelings. In addition the inherent group interaction can allow individuals to explore different roles among their peers, especially those involving leadership and cooperation.

Affective Goals

Certain affective goals might also be better accomplished by an activity centered classroom. If activities focus upon problems pertinent to the students' interest and needs, then the boredom often seen in a teacher centered lecture-discussion class-room can be much less a problem. Too, activity science offers everyone a chance at being successful, even if only in a manipulative way. This success can help to form future positive feelings and attitudes toward science and school in general. As Simpson (1979) states, "Success breeds success."

WHAT KIND OF ACTIVITIES CAN BE DEFINED?

While the general arguments stated above imply that all activities are equally worthwhile, a logical analysis refutes this idea. On one extreme is the recipe lab approach in which students perform a specified sequence of steps, uncritically, to obtain a desired result. Often recipe labs are done to "prove" the truth involved in a statement made by a teacher or textbook. This type of activity does little to stimulate thinking and probably only serves to break up the boredom of listening to the teacher or reading the textbook. At the opposite extreme are activities which begin with a question or problem and ask the students to participate in the solution. The steps to this end are not necessarily set and the answer to the problem is not known in advance. Thinking is a major part of the participation. The active attempt to resolve the question is often more important than getting a correct answer.

Activities which stress the solution over the methods of attaining the solution are generally content oriented; activities which stress the "process" of getting answers generally are process skill development oriented.

The prime focus of the remainder of this article will be process skill activities. A list of these skills usually includes observing, quantifying, identifying and controlling variables, designing experiments, hypothesizing, defining operationally, organizing and collecting data, graphing and generalizing.

THE IMPORTANCE OF PROCESS SKILLS

In addition to the reasons already given for the importance of activities in general, there are several strong arguments for inclusion of process skill activities. One is the generalizability of these skills to life. Many life problems can be analyzed and solutions proposed by applying process skills. Which brand of soap or corn flakes provides the best value? Are frozen, canned or fresh green beans more economical? Should a hydroelectric, coal burning or nuclear plant be built in the local community? Which candidate better reflects an individual's viewpoint? All these questions can be simplified by collecting and organizing data and drawing conclusions from it. The skills of identifying and controlling appropriate variables, designing experiments and defining operationally are all important parts in this process.

Another important reason for including process skill activities is that these activities more accurately reflect the nature of science and the typical activity of scientists. Science is a dynamic enterprise; it is a search for answers. Science is *not* just a collection of facts and conclusions. At any one time the information contained in a "textbook represents only our present conclusions about a body of scientific knowledge" (Hurd, 1970). Most students do not understand the true nature of science as an ongoing and tentative search, unless it is approached as a search and not the solution. Process skill activities provide the perspective necessary for middle school students to begin to view science in this light. Each student will be acting as a scientist. He will be actively observing, hypothesizing, collecting data and experimenting.

Another argument for process skill activities involves the development of formal operational abilities. Piaget operationally defined (through his tasks) several abstract thinking abilities that together comprise formal operations (Inhelder and Piaget, 1958). Prominent among these abilities is the identification and control of variables. "The formal operational thinker inspects his problem data, hypothesizes that such and such a theory or explanation might be the correct one, deduces from it that so and so empirical phenomena ought logically to occur or not occur in reality, and then tests his theory by seeing if these predicted phenomena do in fact occur" (Flavell, 1977). In simpler language a formal thinker can set up and make a fair test, *precisely the same activity involved in performing a process skill experimenting activity*. Although the research is a bit unclear, there appears to be great potential for developing formal reasoning abilities in middle school students through the use of process skill activities over a long period of time.

WHICH PROCESS SKILLS IN MIDDLE SCHOOL?

The major skill to be developed in middle school is conducting a fair experiment or fair test. Many, if not most, of the other process skills can be thought of as components of this superordinate ability. Observing and quantifying are often used for data collection. Hypothesizing, identifying and controlling variables, designing experiments and defining operationally are all parts of setting up a fair experiment. Graphing and generalizing are skills used in interpreting results.

IMPLEMENTING PROCESS SKILL ACTIVITIES

The first step necessary for implementing process skill activities is choosing an appropriate unit topic. Some topics can more naturally involve students in collecting and analyzing data. Others, while they might be of great scientific interest or of interest to a particular science teacher, do not provide appropriate opportunities for manipulating materials and variables. Units involving measurement of certain aspects of the five senses or those stressing pollution assessment in the local school area or measurement of local weather conditions with home-made devices can work exceedingly well. Others such as theoretical electricity, atoms and molecules, and black holes are extremely difficult.

Topics which stress abstract properties or laws are more difficult for middle school students for at least two reasons. First it is often difficult to identify concrete experiences or activities that can lead to process skill development. Either the activities themselves or the conclusions that are to be drawn involve abstractions that are difficult for students to grasp. Secondly, research has so far shown that only formal operational students (thus not many middle school students) appear to truly understand abstract concepts taught via traditional lecture-discussion techniques (Lawson and Renner, 1975). Even more disappointing is the tentative finding that the use of illustrations, diagrams and physical models helps only the formal students (Cantu and Herron, 1978). While these studies used secondary students as subjects, the implications for middle school students appear to be clear. If one desires to develop process skill abilities, the avoidance of abstract topics as a vehicle is important. There are enough interesting and significant concrete topics available to middle school teachers so that this should not prove exceedingly difficult.

After unit topics are selected, the students must be given opportunities to practice the process skills. If process skill activities are new to students, then skills such as observing, graphing, collecting data, using tables, forming appropriate hypotheses and operationally defining variables should probably be practiced individually before being combined in a true experiment. Initial training should also stress appropriate strategies for mastery of these process skills. For example, brainstorming techniques can work well for identifying variables and defining operationally. A check of the brainstormed variable lists would also indicate whether all variables have been controlled except the manipulated and responding variables. Soon students should be combining these separate skills and performing the superordinate skill of conducting a fair test.

Initially fair test activities should involve relatively simple or familiar problems. Situations involving a small number of variables and which deal with commonplace problems within the students' environment are important starting points. After a reasonable facility with singular skills and simpler problems is attained, then the teacher can proceed slowly to more complex situations.

CONDUCTING A FAIR EXPERIMENT—SOME EXAMPLES
The Sense of Touch

The first step in setting up a fair experiment is asking an appropriate question. Many such questions can be posed relative to the sense of touch.

- How accurate is touch in telling temperature?
- How far apart are touch receptors?
- Are some parts of the body more receptive to touch than others?
- Are some individuals more receptive to touch than others?
- Is the hair on the neck as sensitive to touch as leg or arm hair?

One of these questions must then be chosen and an appropriate hypothesis formed, for example, neck hair is more sensitive to touch than either leg or arm hair.

Variables must then be identified, perhaps by brainstorming a list of those which might affect the hypothesis. The manipulated or independent variable (e.g., type of hair) and the responding or dependent variable (e.g., sensitivity to touch) must be chosen. Both of these variables must then be operationally defined so that they can be measured. This can be accomplished using brainstorming techniques again. To continue the example, one appropriate operational definition for sensitivity to touch might be the ability to perceive touch. Type of hair might be operationally defined as hair on different parts of the body, e.g., the arm, neck, head or leg. All other appropriate variables should be controlled, if possible. In our example the instrument used to touch the hair, the pressure applied to each hair and the number of hairs touched could and should be standardized. A sharpened pencil, the lightest possible touch and one hair could be the operational definitions of the controlled variables.

Once variables have been identified and operationally defined an experimental design must be chosen. How many trials should be performed? In what order should the tests occur? What specific data should be recorded? Questions like these must be answered before data can be collected and organized. Five trials and a staggered order of testing the body parts might be appropriate for our example. These choices allow for experimental error and a fair comparison of different body parts. Once the design is chosen, the data collection can begin.

Data organization can be expedited with middle school students by discussing a suitable table before data collection begins. At first the teacher might recommend an appropriate table, however, students should soon be suggesting their own. Class data might be further organized by using a class chart upon which all results are placed. This allows for a smooth transition from data organizing to the important step of generalizing. One significant aspect of this step is that generalizations can take many forms. Certainly some investigations provide relatively clean results which allow for a statement of the relationship between the manipulated and responding variables, for example, neck hair is more sensitive to touch than either arm or leg hair. Other types of generalizations simply pose further questions to be answered through future experiments, for example, would neck hair still prove more sensitive if more than one hair were touched each time? This second type of generalization is very important if middle school students are to begin to understand the true nature of science. Teachers must not only allow further questions, but encourage them.

Dandelions

A simple flower or weed such as the dandelion can provide another example for generating a fair experiment. Several appropriate questions are possible.

- What proportion of dandelion seeds will germinate in a wet paper towel?
- How does temperature affect the germination rate of the seeds?
- Will pre-soaking or refrigeration of dandelion seeds affect their germination rate?

Once a question is chosen, a hypothesis is formulated, e.g., a temperature above 25° C will adversely affect germination rate. Appropriate variables must then be identified:

- Manipulated variable (e.g., temperature)
- Responding variable (e.g., germination rate)
- Controlled variable (e.g., amount of water, age of seeds, etc.)

Each variable must then be operationally defined.

The experiment must then be designed. How many and which temperatures will be tested? How long should the seeds be subjected to a particular temperature? What length of time will be allowed for germination? After these questions are answered and the design is set, the data can be collected and organized using charts or graphs. Generalizations from the organized data in the form of conclusions or questions can then be made.

Other Questions

Once the above method is somewhat internalized, performing a fair test becomes a matter of generating appropriate questions through which the process skills can be further practiced. Examples of appropriate questions for consumer affairs and the senses are listed below. It is important to note that many researchable questions can be generated from other appropriate, concrete topics.

Consumer Affairs

- Does one fast food chain provide more meat in a hamburger than others?
- Is one brand of paper towel stronger than the others? or more absorbant?
- Will one brand of dishwasher liquid wash more dishes per unit cost?
- Is it more economical to buy boneless meat or a piece with the bone in?
- Does one brand of antacid neutralize more acid than the others?

The Senses
- What factors affect the blinking rate of various individuals?
- How does the sense of sight or smell affect taste?
- What effect does the sense of sight have on hearing?
- Is the minimum threshold for hearing different for certain individuals?
- How does the size of the outer ear affect the hearing threshold for individuals?

SOME FINAL CONSIDERATIONS

Many teachers have erroneously inferred that a ceaseless array of activities is best for middle school students. However, teachers wishing to implement a productive, activity centered classroom need to spend an adequate amount of time explaining, discussing and integrating activity results. Activities, by themselves, confer no magical understanding to all children. Teachers must help students by spending the necessary class time getting students to make sense of their experiences and by helping them connect activities to past and future science knowledge.

REFERENCES

Cantu, L. & Herron, D. Concrete and formal Piagetian stages and science concept attainment. *Journal of Research in Science Teaching*, 1978, *15*, 135-143.

Chiapetta, E. A review of Piagetian studies relevant to science instruction at the secondary and college level. *Science Education*, 1976, *60*, 253-261.

Elementary Science Study, *The Ess Reader,* Newton, MA: Education Development Center, Inc., 1970.

Flavell, J. *Cognitive Development*, Englewood Cliffs, NJ: Prentice-Hall, Inc., 1977.

Georgiady, N.P. & Romano, L.G. Growth characteristics of middle school children: curriculum implications. *Middle School Journal*, 1977, 12-23.

Hurd, P.D. *New Curriculum Perspectives for Junior High School Science*. Belmont, CA: Wadsworth Publishing Co., 1970.

Inhelder, B. & Piaget, J. *The Growth of Logical Thinking From Childhood to Adolescence*, New York: Basic Books, Inc., 1958.

Lawson, A. & Renner, J. Relationships of science subject matter and developmental levels of learners. *Journal of Research in Science Teaching*, 1975, *12*, 347-358.

Lovell, K. A follow-up study of Inhelder and Piaget's the Growth of Logical Thinking. British Journal of Psychology, 1961, *52*, 143-153.

Piaget, J. Intellectual evaluation from adolescence to adult. *Human Development*, 1972, *15*, 1-12. Renner, J., Grant, R. & Sutherland, J. Content and concrete thought. *Science Education*, 1978, *62*, 215-221.

Schwebel, M. & Raph, J. *Piaget in the Classroom*, New York: Basic Books, Inc., 1973.

Simpson, R.D. Breeding success in science. *The Science Teacher*, 1979, *46*, 24-26.

Graphing

Michael J. Padilla
Danny L. McKenzie

Methods of condensing and interpreting data are becoming increasingly necessary for intelligent survival. Yet, producing graphs and interpreting data from them does not come easily to most students. There is an abstract quality in stating the relationship between two variables from a line drawn on a paper. Indeed, a recent study found a .77 correlation between formal reasoning ability and graphing skills. (2)* Certainly more research is necessary before teaching methods and ideas, shaped to individual developmental needs, can be produced. Meanwhile, the classroom teacher, dealing with early adolescents involved in process skill activities which include data collection, needs effective methodologies that can be used today.

PREREQUISITE KNOWLEDGE

Many kinds of two-dimensional graphs are appropriate for early adolescents from bar graphs and histograms to line graphs. But what does a student need to know *before* he or she can graph? One prerequisite is learning the difference between responding and manipulated variables. Graphs describe the relationship between a variable that was manipulated (e.g., the amount of water given to a plant) and another that responds (e.g., plant growth) to the manipulated variable. Students should identify both types of variables from a description of an experiment. (3)

A second prerequisite skill is the ability to construct and read a data table. The manipulated variable is always placed on the left hand side of the table. Values of this variable are organized in either ascending or descending order. Values of the responding variable are recorded in the right hand column and must correspond to the appropriate value of the manipulated variable. Students can practice constructing data tables and graphs by collecting their own data.

BAR GRAPHS AND HISTOGRAMS

Because of their simplicity, bar graphs and histograms are the logical choices for introducing graphing. Bar graphs usually display the occurrence of two or more objects or events (e.g., apple and orange production in 1980). Histograms generally display the occurrence of one object or event through a continuum, such as time (e.g., apple production over a period of ten years). In bar graphs, the bars are separated from each other by spaces. Eliminating the spaces between bars in a histogram facilitates identification of trends.

Constructing axes is a basic step in both bar graphs and histograms. Remember that the categories under examination are located on the horizontal axis and the frequency of occurrence is located on the vertical axis. Remind students to label

---

*See References.

properly each axis and to make the widths of the bars constant so they do not appear to be of different values.

Finally, students should include a descriptive title to complete their graphs. Titles should allow other students to interpret graphs without additional information.

LINE GRAPHS

Axis construction for line graphs is similar to that of histograms. The manipulated variable appears on the horizontal axis; the responding variable on the vertical axis. Label each with the variable being measured and the units used to measure the variable.

Next assign a numerical scale to each axis. The scale must include the entire range of values for the particular variable. Students may subtract the smallest value of the variable from the largest value. Next, divide the difference by five and round off the answer to the nearest whole number. This number becomes the interval for the scale.

Plotting points is important for correct graph construction. Some students, however, have difficulty keeping imaginary lines straight. Using two rulers or dashed lines to locate the proper point may be helpful.

Next, construct a best fit line which approximates the trend of the data points. It is *not* a dot-to-dot connection. Rather, it is a line among the data points which represents the general relationship between the variables. Equal numbers of points should fall on each side of the best fit line. This step might prove difficult at first, but is helpful in data interpretation.

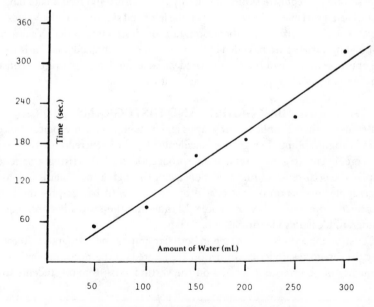

Time necessary to heat different amounts of water 10° C.

94

INTERPRETING LINE GRAPHS

Interpreting line graphs is perhaps the most important—and the most difficult—step of all. Begin with simple straight line relationships. Try having students use the same sentence format for verbally interpreting graphs. An example is, "As the (manipulated variable) increases, the (responding variable) increases/decreases." For example, in an experiment which tests the time (responding variable) it takes to heat different amounts of water (manipulated variable) to a specific temperature, a student might conclude, "As the amount of water to be heated increases, the amount of time needed to heat the water increases." More complicated relationships where the values of the responding variable decrease as the manipulated variable increases should not be introduced until simpler relationships are mastered.

Curvilinear graphs are more difficult to interpret. For example, in an experiment that measures the effect of different amounts of water (manipulated variable) on plant growth (responding variable), an upside down U-shaped graph is constructed. Students must use a compound sentence to interpret the graph. For example, "As the amount of water increases from 0 to 30 mL per day, the plant growth increased, and after 30 mL per day, the plant growth decreased." Again, by using a similar sentence structure each time, the student will begin to learn the meaning behind the words.

Graphing skills are important to success in many school subjects. Science offers a unique opportunity to practice these skills in a meaningful context. However, teachers must be aware that certain students will have difficulty especially with interpreting relationships between variables. To best help students, go slowly from simple to complex and provide many opportunities for practice.

REFERENCES

1. Funk, H., J. Okey, R. Fiel, H. Jaus, and C. Sprague. *Learning Science Process Skills*. Kendall-Hunt Publishing Company, Dubuque, IA. 1979.
2. Padilla, M., J. Okey, and F. G. Dillashaw. "The Relationship Between Science Process Skill and Formal Thinking Abilities." Paper presented at the National Association for Research in Science Teaching Annual Meeting, New York City. April 1981.
3. Padilla, M. "Using Consumer Science to Develop Experimental Techniques." *Science and Children* 18:22-23; January 1981.

Using Consumer Science to Develop Experimental Techniques

Michael J. Padilla

One way to develop a scientifically literate society is to cultivate in the young the abilities involved in scientific thinking processes; i.e., the abilities to identify, control and define variables, to construct hypotheses, to collect, graph, and interpret data, and to make generalizations. Middle-school youngsters do not master integrated process skills easily, however. Many find this type of thinking "unnatural," perhaps because they usually think in concrete terms. Often they do not see the connection between experimenting and the real world. Thus, it is a major function of the middle school science teacher to give students multiple experiences with process skills using simple, highly relevant problems. Consumer science is useful for introducing many of the integrated process skills and is a simple and relevant topic area.

A FAIR EXPERIMENT

First consider the methods of conducting a fair experiment or test. Students must choose a question to be investigated. One consumer science example is "How does the amount of detergent used affect stains in clothing?" Have students identify variables relevant to the question and designate the manipulated variable, the responding variable, and the controlled variable. In the example, the amount of detergent is the manipulated variable. Students might choose three or more amounts to test. The degree to which a certain kind of stain is removed by the detergent is the responding variable. Variables to be controlled are the amount of water to be mixed with the detergent, the amount of "washing action" to be applied, the type of stain to be removed, and others. Each of the variables must be operationally defined so students can measure them. In the example, defining 30, 60, and 90 milliliters (mL) of detergent is an appropriate operational definition.

Students should next organize the experiment. How many trials are necessary? Which specific amounts of detergent should be tested? How long should the material be washed? Students must answer these questions and others so that a fair procedure is followed.

Once students have organized the experiment, they can collect and display data on bar graphs and simple data tables or make frequency counts. Students just learning to experiment may find line graphs difficult to interpret; they should use other methods in the beginning. Data display techniques are important because they facilitate the next important step in an experiment—generalizing. Learning that both over generalization and under generalization can lead to errors and that further questions and experiments are often the only result of an investigation are important steps in understanding the nature of experimentation.

Refining individual skills apart from an experiment may be necessary at first, but the sooner students experience the entire process, as in the above example, the more relevant and easily understood that process will be. Autonomous use of these skills might take many months (or even longer) for middle school students to acquire. What is important is that teachers supply nonfrustrating opportunities for students to practice the skills over the school year. Acquisition will come with time.

CONSUMER TESTING FAST FOOD CHAINS

The fast food chain can provide opportunities for conducting a fair experiment. Students can compare hamburgers in many ways. For example, how does the amount of a hamburger from chain A compare to that of chain B? How does the weight per unit cost of hamburger compare? Before cooking? After cooking? What percent of total weight of the hamburger is the meat, the bun, the filler?

Each of these questions can be investigated using procedures similar to those already outlined. To test the question of which chain serves the "best" hamburgers, students might perform separate experiments or collect data on various facets of hamburger excellence. A tally of points accumulated in each category would indicate an overall winner.

Students can compare other food items. They can measure which chain gives the greatest weight or volume of french fries per unit cost and the relative economy of small, medium and large orders of fries. They can compare greasiness by spreading the fries over paper towels and weighing the towels before and after to obtain the weight of absorbed grease. Students can measure the amount of salt by soaking the french fries in water for a short time and then evaporating the water and weighing the remaining salt. Cherry pies can be compared on a cost basis or by counting the number of cherries supplied in each pie. They can test shakes for taste. If they warm them so that the air whipped into the shakes dissipates, the true volume of the liquid can also be compared.

Teachers should point out the subtle difference between the manipulated variable in the detergent example and that in the fast food examples. Technically, the experimenter is not manipulating the values of the independent variable in the latter example, but only choosing values that already exist (e.g., the weight of the hamburger). While this makes only a small difference in how the experiment is conducted, it might cause some logical difficulties for the more precise and brighter students.

OTHER EXAMPLES

Testing product claims such as "absorbs more water than any other paper towel" or "cleans as it disinfects" provides opportunities for many good experiments. As avid TV watchers, the students can suggest many products to be tested. Here are a few statements to verify about soap as topics for exploration:

- Facial soap A leaves the skin softer and more youthful than soap B.
- Deodorant soap A surpasses deodorant soaps B, C, and D in eliminating odors.
- Dishwashing liquid A cuts grease more effectively than all others available in the same color.

- Dishwashing liquid A is gentler on the hands than liquids B and C.
- Shampoo A mends split ends better than its competitors.
- Shampoo A produces more suds than shampoo B.
- Liquid detergents wash clothes more effectively than granular detergents.

With a bit of creative brainstorming, teachers and students can identify other consumer problems and develop processes for fair experiments. Good luck and good experimenting!

Art by Lydia Nolan-Davis

Focusing on the Senses

Michael J. Padilla

Adolescence is a transition between childhood and adulthood. Rapid growth and maturation often lead to awkwardness and self-consciousness among middle and junior high school students. More important from a student's perspective is that the onset of adolescence coincides with an intense interest in the peer group and how "I" fit into that group. Questions like "Am I different from others my age?" "Why can't I control the pitch of my voice?" and "Will I ever develop bumps and curves the others have?" are the heart of reality for early adolescents. Working against or ignoring this behavior can cross teachers' and students' purposes. As Nancy Griffin stated in the first "Early Adolescence" article (*Science and Children*, September 1980), "Nothing the teacher can do will change to any significant degree the special priorities of this age group."

If teachers accept the inevitability of self-centered behavior, the only sensible solution is to try to match the science curriculum to the special needs of middle school students. One important aspect of this match should emphasize activities. Physical movement, as well as the group interaction skills necessary for a cooperative venture, are important types of learning for early adolescents. A second vital component is studying science topics which are meaningful to the early adolescents, for instance ecology, pollution, consumer science, and energy. The theme of this article, the senses, is meaningful, has the potential to help students learn about themselves and their bodies, and will strengthen their process skill abilities.

A unit on the senses offers students an opportunity to be involved in many kinds of activities like conducting experiments, developing models, and collecting and displaying data. Science content about how the eyes, ears, nose, tongue, and skin transmit sensation to the brain is plentiful.

Uniquely, the senses offer a personal opportunity for early adolescents to explore their own attributes. The concepts of variation and "normality" naturally flow from these explorations, leading to a better understanding of "what is happening to me" and "how I fit in with the others." Don't overlook the many opportunities a senses unit will offer for fun in the classroom either.

SIGHT

Using standard eye charts and color blindness tests, students can successfully test their own eyesight. These tests are available from the local public health service or an optometrist. Investigate peripheral vision capacity by measuring the point at which a student can see the upright thumb of his or her outstretched arm moved slowly from the side to the front of the head. Likewise, determine depth perception by having students identify which one of a pair of pencils is in front of the other when held closely together at a distance of six meters (m). Measure the minimum difference in depth that can be perceived by both one and two eyes. These activities will need planning to insure fair tests, correct data collection, and recording

99

methods. Be sensitive to individuals with extreme scores, acknowledging the expectation that most individuals will vary from the average.

Content-oriented activities emphasizing the parts and functions of the eye and how lenses can be used to correct common eye problems also are easily incorporated. Compare the parts of the eye which parallel those parts of a simple camera. Observe how the iris reacts to light and dark and how the upside down image of a birthday candle is reflected on the retina. To expand the study, have a local optometrist or opthomologist demonstrate how lenses correct typical eye problems.

TOUCH

Touch also offers opportunities for sense activities. Map the locations of receptors for different sensations like hot, cold, pain, and pressure on the forearm or the back of the hand. Collect mapping data by drawing a 4 × 4 centimeter (cm) grid on the forearm and testing each square with the head or point of a pin. As data for the entire class are compiled, patterns emerge that imply there are different receptors for each type of "feel." Research in reference books can offer background information on the types, relative positions, and number of different receptors. Further exploration with touch can compare the relative sensitivity of different parts of the body. Are fingertips, the forearm, the lower part of the leg, or the back of the neck more sensitive to cold, to heat, to pressure, or to pain? What is the minimum distance over which students can feel both prongs of a paper clip bent in a "U" shape? Does this vary from one body part to another? These questions provide excellent problems for research.

SMELL

Measure the amount of time necessary for a strong smell (like perfume) to travel various distances and directions in the classroom. Construct a model for dispersing scents to determine the nature of aromas and how they travel.

Identifying common substances by smell is a fun activity and good experience in observation, description, and classification. It is not tied to the sense of sight. Use common household items like cinnamon, vinegar, garlic, oranges, peanut butter, coffee, and perfume. Develop a smell classification system that groups individual items.

TASTE

Ask blindfolded students (care should be taken to avoid transmitting germs of the eye by using separate blindfolds or tissue liners) to identify several foods by taste, both with and without the aid of their sense of smell. Use foods like apples, pears, and potatoes because their similar textures will challenge students. As with smell, various foods can be identified by taste and classified into broad groups.

Test parts of the tongue (back, front, and both sides) to determine which is sensitive to each of the four basic tastes. Prepare water solutions of vinegar (sour), salt (salty), sugar (sweet), and aspirin (bitter). With a fresh toothpick, apply minute quantities of each to the four parts of the tongue. Rinse the mouth with water after each taste. Again, the experiences of collecting data, using properly constructed tables, and generalizing results from the data are meaningful process skill activities.

Art by *Lydia Nolan-Davis*

HEARING

Hearing can be tested much like sight except that a specific noise must provide the stimulus. Move a ticking clock or a metronome toward and away from each student to establish the maximum distance they can hear the sound. Eliminate extraneous classroom noises for this investigation to be meaningful. To test dependency of hearing on sight, have blindfolded students point in the direction of a sound or name the direction of a sound when using only one ear. Measure the effects of extraneous classroom noises for this investigation to be meaningful. To test dependency of hearing on sight, have blindfolded students point in the direction of a sound observation, have students identify mystery sounds from an audio tape you have made. Most important in studying the senses is placing the emphasis on the individuals, and how one individual normally varies from others. A well-constructed senses unit can accomplish this major goal and other goals in process, content, and affective areas.

REFERENCES

1. Burkman, E., et al. *Investigating Variation*. Intermediate Science Curriculum Study. Silver Burdett Co., Morristown, New Jersey. 1977.
2. Katagiri, G., Trojack D., and Brown, D. *You and Me*. Self-Paced Investigation for Elementary Science. Silver Burdett Co., Morristown, New Jersey. 1976.
3. Stecher, A., et al. *Your Senses*. Examining Your Environment Series. Holt, Rinehart and Winston of Canada, Limited, Toronto. 1976.

Science Bowl Stirs School Spirit

Karen E. Reynolds

The final whistle blows, and the Havenscourt Junior High auditorium fills with cheers and applause. A team sporting the name of "The Professors" has won the annual Science Bowl!

For years, ninth-grade science students at Havenscourt have presented the Science Bowl as a school- and community-wide assembly, a science event which combines academics with the kind of spirit usually reserved for sports events.

"Tradition" has long played in our Science Bowl's favor. First, after an initial investment of time and effort to establish procedures and make basic supporting props, only minor adjustments are required in years following. And second, the event has gained in prestige over the years, so that it is now a highlight to which students look forward—especially during the year of their active participation. This coming spring will be our thirteenth annual Science Bowl.

Presentation of the Science Bowl as a public event involves a number of direct and indirect benefits to students, including the following:

- In preparing for the competition, students review course content;
- Science is seen as worthy of being "on stage," and students receive experience in helping with a theatrical production;
- Members of the audience can feel a part of the action as they attempt to answer questions for themselves and keep up with the score;
- Parents, other community members, teachers outside the department, and administrators are invited to attend or to participate as officials;
- Because the event represents a special time for science to "go public," it provides the opportunity for our department to make awards to students or adults who have been particularly active in or supportive of the science program.

Havenscourt's first Science Bowl, in 1968, was patterned after TV's College Bowl; it involved panels of students, competing to answer objective-type questions. Score was kept on a chalkboard, a series of bells and buzzers provided a "quiz show" atmosphere, and students cheered vigorously for their favorite team. Over the years, we have added a scoreboard with readable numbered cards, lights to accompany the bells and buzzers, a considerable amount of stage art, and practical "roll-on" challenges to be included with the verbal questions. The following are our rules and procedures.

CONTEST RULES AND PROCEDURES

1. There are two periods of playing time. The first and second halves are each 15 minutes in length, with a four-minute rest period between halves.
2. In front of each team member there is a button. When a button is pressed—indicating that that person thinks he or she knows an answer—a bell sounds and a light flashes. These special effects signal which team is to have the first opportunity to answer the question.

3. A toss-up question, which either team may answer, is asked at the beginning of each round of the game. The student signalling first has the opportunity to answer that question for his team. Any team member having the answer may give a response: In fact, the toss-up is the only time in the game when a contestant may answer without consulting with team members. After the signal, the answer must be given within five seconds.

4. If a team gives an incorrect answer to the toss-up question, ten points are deducted from its score. The question is re-read if necessary, and the other team given an opportunity to answer. No penalty is assessed the second team if it cannot answer or if it gives an incorrect answer. However, for either team, a correct answer on the toss-up merits 25 points, plus a chance at a bonus question.

5. After a correct toss-up answer, a multi-part bonus question is asked. The team is allowed a maximum of 20 seconds to confer on the question. Team members may take notes and transmit them to the captain. Only the captain may announce answers for the team on bonus questions, each of which contains two to five parts, each worth five points.

6. The winning team is determined by the total number of points for both periods of play.

ALL FOR ONE AND . . .

Teams may be comprised of entire science classes or of smaller special-interest groups. Since only two teams may compete at a time, playoffs can be held whenever more than two teams are initially eligible for competition.

There are a variety of different jobs for students to do. Four to eight students (including one captain) are typically chosen as potential stage panelists, though only four may play at any one time. (Substitutions are allowed at halftime.) Students may also coach and create practice questions, or they may make signs for the team.

Student assistants who belong to neither team help plan the event, make the main stage banner, act as scorekeepers or stage assistants, usher, or write invitations to guests and officials, and send follow-up thank-you notes.

Two kinds of questions are used throughout the competition:

- *Objective questions* calling for factual information, such as "What is the speed of light, in metric?"
- *Practical challenges* ("roll-ons") involving use of apparatus or visual aids; these are rolled out to the center of the stage on a cart. Example: Given a ring stand, pulleys, weights, and string, students (one from each team) race to "lift the weight."

Adult officials include a scorekeeper, a timer, a moderator (who reads questions), and an "expert" to interpret answers when needed. An adult is also stationed backstage to assist with the preparation of "roll-ons" if necessary. Participating adults often become "regulars" who look forward to serving each year.

Awards are presented at the conclusion of the competition and include a "perpetual trophy" on which winning team names are inscribed each year, plus individual ribbons for team panelists. Often an administrator or community member is honored with the task of presenting awards.

Science Olympics
(Or Science for the Sport of It)
Carey W. Fletcher

Teenagers enjoy competition—especially if it is fun and if the winners receive prizes. This motivation, coupled with proper planning, is the key to organizing olympic games in science, where junior or senior high school students can enter events based on scientific principles, measurements, or equipment.

Last spring at Charlotte Junior-Senior High School, an inner city school in Rochester, New York, I coordinated science olympic games that were successful not only because students enjoyed themselves, but also because the program fostered a more positive attitude toward the school's science program. In addition, publicity in the local news media raised the students' morale and, hence, school spirit.

CHOOSING THE EVENTS

Teachers can choose many kinds of events for such a contest. Selection should depend on the background, ability, and maturity of the students. Some suggestions, developed at Charlotte Junior-Senior High, are:

Egg drop. Can an egg be dropped, without breaking, from a second story window? Protective materials surrounding the egg can weigh no more than 600 g; parachutes are allowed. Each contestant multiplies the shortest longitudinal axis of his or her device times its mass times its dropping time. The student with the lowest product wins.

Paper airplane engineering. Students design paper airplanes that are tested for flying accuracy (through a hula hoop) and distance along a straight path (with deviations from the path subtracted from the distance flown).

Paper tower building. Students use one sheet of ditto paper (8½″ × 11″), scissors, and 50 cm of tape to build a free-standing tower in only five minutes.

Bottle music. The contestant must play a tune by blowing through a "musical scale" of pop bottles filled with varying amounts of water. (Judging, of course, is somewhat subjective.)

Prediction. Students predict where a steel ball—riding on a runway made from a curved piece of V-tubing—will land.

Bike balance. Students must ride a bike as slowly as possible between two strips of tape, each 25 m long and positioned 75 cm apart, without touching the lines. The winner is the student who completes the course in the slowest time while managing to avoid taking a spill from the bike.

Bike slalom. Participants bicycle first along one side of a row of objects in a zigzag arrangement, then along the other side. The winner is the student who finishes the course in the shortest time.

Bottoms up. How fast can contestants empty the contents of a 2-liter glass bottle into another container without spilling any liquid?

Apartment building. Using 26 playing cards, competitors construct the highest free-standing "apartment high rise" they can in five minutes.

Light-handed slalom race. Carrying Ping-Pong balls in teaspoons, runners must weave in and out around obstacles in a zigzag course as rapidly as possible, without dropping the balls.

Bridge building. Students design and build a bridge using glue and balsa wood weighing no more than 100 g. The bridge capable of supporting the heaviest weight wins.

Refraction prediction. A beam of light (preferably a laser beam) is directed at an angle through a semi-circular, transparent object (solid or filled with water). After the beam passes through the object, it first hits a triangular glass prism at an angle and then is refracted onto a screen. The winner is the student who most nearly predicts the spot where the light will land on the screen.

BEHIND THE SCENES

Organizing science olympic games requires the cooperation of all teachers in the science department and the assistance of perhaps 15 to 20 students. The following points should be considered in planning the project:

- Publicity: Advertise the science olympic games in class; in the school news bulletin; over the public address system; through flyers posted in the halls and the cafeteria; and even in local newsletters, newspapers, and on radio and television stations.
- Setup and cleanup: The teacher or student responsible for an event should also be responsible for acquiring any necessary equipment and setting it up. Teachers and students who set up the olympics should also take charge of the cleanup effort afterward.
- "Thank-you" committee: Appoint several persons to write notes of appreciation to businesses or organizations that donated prizes and to anyone who helped make the project a success.
- Monitors: Have one or more teachers posted as necessary to keep order among participants as well as observers.
- Scorekeepers: Assign persons to tally points and determine the winners quickly.
- Name tags and registration. For the sake of orderliness and convenience, each participant should be issued a name tag when registering. At our olympics, registration was limited to the first 150 students who paid a 25-cent registration fee. The fee ensured the sincerity of each entrant and helped defray costs.

THE FINISH LINE

Based on the philosophy that every student who successfully completes an event deserves recognition, a minimum of one point was awarded to those who "just finished" our olympic events; two points to those with an average performance; and three points to those whose performance was above average. At the end of each event, additional points were awarded to those placing first through fifth.

In the end, the greatest reward from organizing our science olympics program came from the many excited students who expressed the hope that the competition would become an annual affair.

The Day We Hung Eighth Grade

Nancy C. Griffin

I'll plead guilty to temporary insanity, but what teacher wouldn't suffer mid-summer madness if asked to teach physical science to eighth-graders in a summer school classroom without air conditioning—and in Florida!

A math colleague and I were at wit's end after only a week of summer school. It seemed impossible to grab hold of students' attention. Our backs to the wall, we confessed (partially facetiously) to an occasional impulse to "hang" the entire eighth grade. Gradually, we became "absorbed" in our fantasy. Could it be that by bodily involving our students in science, we could motivate them to learn science?

When we announced gravely to the students that they were to be hung, the class responded with sarcastic groans and jeers. "You're crazy," they protested, "you can't hang us."

On the appointed day, students were reluctant and grumbly, but they followed us rather docilely to the gymnasium where we had set up some stout ropes and protective mats. (We had also advised them to wear jeans.) No one wanted to be hung. So the math teacher and I explained in detail how we would pinpoint their centers of gravity by hanging them from various angles, dropping a "plumbob" at each position, and then determining where the lines of the plumbob intersected.

Once we had actually located a reluctant volunteer, interest perked up. Questions from the class came fast. "What does 'center of gravity' mean?" "Of what use is gravity?" For the moment we declined to answer. As the period drew to a close and the class became more insistent, we put away the equipment and began to discuss the significance of what had been demonstrated. "Does center of gravity play a role in sports?" "Does it differ in men and women? Why?" "How does it influence balance?" As many questions as possible were answered through demonstrations. The class was an overwhelming success. Despite the heat, we couldn't get rid of the students. They stayed after class to be hung again, to ask more questions, to compare centers of gravity.

THROWING YOURSELF INTO IT

Since total body involvement seemed our key to success, we decided to incorporate body experiments into all of the middle school science and math classes.

Drowning (or finding one's volume by water displacement) was the next step. Unable to locate a secondhand bathtub, we borrowed instead a child's plastic wading pool. We added 20 liters of water to the pool, marked the water's edge, and continued marking after every additional three liters until the pool was filled. Then we removed an appropriate amount of water so the pool would not overflow when a child submerged himself. Finding how much the water rose when a child was submerged allowed us to calculate his volume in liters.

In another body experiment, weight was calculated by "dangling" a student from a spring scale. Knowing both body volume and mass, it was thus possible for students to discover how dense they really were!

Eighth-graders who had worked with mass, volume, and density in the regular school term did not seem to understand these ideas well before the body experiments. After having been bodily involved, however, they found the terms had new meaning—a fact we sensed in classroom discussions and were able to substantiate using pre- and posttests.

By now, students were asking, "What's next?", parents were visiting and calling to praise our ideas, and we were racking our brains to think of more ways to have body involvement.

Creating human pendulums gave us an opportunity to introduce the concept of hypothesis. Before the activity, we asked the class to predict which of several types of pendulums (such as long or short, light or heavy weights, etc.) would have the fastest period. Most predictions were wrong. And even after some of the various human pendulums had been swung, arguments persisted; students insisted we had not been accurate and that our results were wrong. We repeated the experiment several times, using various human pendulums before the results were totally accepted.

A PROGRAM IS BORN

Our students learned a good deal through these experiences, but we learned more. Early on it became apparent to us that enthusiasm generates motivation—and that enthusiasm grows out of changing student activities frequently and imaginatively.

We expanded on this approach to learning science in subsequent semesters, eventually producing a unified science program for the sixth, seventh, and eighth grades which we call Interrelated Explorations in Science. The program minimizes the traditional fences separating one science from another, and presents content through four major conceptual themes (quantification, orderliness, change, and equilibrium). Throughout, we use games, dramatizations, bulletin boards, and gimmicks of all kinds.

We've learned our lesson well—middle school students learn most successfully when both their minds and bodies are active. And kids are never more active than when they're "hanging around"!

Energy Consumption, Calculate It!

Howard Munson

Each year more new electrical gadgets for the home appear on the market. Many of the gadgets, or appliances, are designed to make meal preparation easier.

A few years ago a popular item was the small toaster-oven, made with top and bottom heat coils designed for baking a small casserole or two or three large potatoes, cooking a small roast, and toasting two slices of bread. Recently, microwave ovens have been promoted as energy savers. Except for toasting bread, microwave ovens do most things regular ovens and toaster ovens do at a faster rate. Also on the market are burger fryers, hotdog cookers, slowcooking pots, self-contained deep fat fryers, and electric woks. These devices do single tasks that can be done on conventional kitchen ranges.

There is no simple nor single answer to whether small appliances conserve or waste energy. There are a number of activities that may help answer the question with respect to individual appliances. This article includes several activities that interest middle-grade students and may stimulate discussion about energy conservation between students and their parents.

THE BURGER PROBLEM

As an introductory example, consider the problem of frying two hamburger patties. There are three electric methods of frying hamburgers: in a frying pan on the electric range; an electric frypan (25-cm square); or a burger-maker. Which method is least costly in terms of energy need?

Two factors are important: (1) the number of watts of electrical power drawn by each appliance and (2) the time it takes to cook hamburgers on each appliance. Watts times time in hours (w × h) equal watt hours. One thousand watt hours is a kilowatt hour. Since electrical power is purchased by the kilowatt hour, electricity consumption is usually described in kilowatt hours.

A large 20-cm diameter electric stove burner uses 1100 watts. Assume that after three minutes of preheating, it takes 10 minutes to cook two burgers, using about 238 watt hours (1100 w × 13/60 hr = 238 wh), or 0.238 kwh.

An electric frypan about 25 cm across uses 1200 watts. After five minutes of preheating, it takes 17 minutes to cook the burgers, using 444 watt hours or 0.444 kwh.

A single burger fryer requires five minutes to preheat, fries the burger in two minutes after which a second burger can be fried immediately. Only nine minutes are required, and since the burger fryer uses 400 watts, 60 watt hours or 0.06 kwh are used. Compare the following examples:

Large burner:

1100 w × 13/60 hr = 238 ÷ 1000 = 0.238 kwh

Frypan:

1200 w × 22/60 hr = 444 ÷ 1000 = 0.444 kwh

Burger-fryer:

400 w × 9/60 hr = 60 ÷ 1000 = 0.06 kwh

Which method consumes the least energy? Obviously, it is the single burger fryer. Are all small appliances similarly efficient or is this a unique situation? Here are some other comparisons to make.

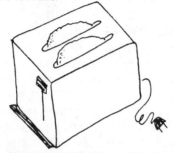

THE TOASTING DILEMMA

Compare three methods for toasting 12 slices of bread—a toaster oven which accepts two slices of bread; a two-slice electric toaster; and a four-slice toaster. From the literature accompanying a home appliance or mail order catalog find the wattage for each appliance and record it.

Assume that the following figures are accurate for time required to toast bread: toaster oven, two minutes; two-slice toaster, two minutes; four-slice toaster, 2.5 minutes. Fill in the blanks below and make the necessary calculations.

Toaster oven:

____ watts × 2/60 hours = ____ watt hours

____ wh × 6 (for 12 slices) = ____ wh

____ wh ÷ 1000 = ____ kilowatt hours

Two-slice toaster:

____ w × 2/60 hr = ____ wh

____ wh × 6 (for 12 slices) = ____ wh

____ wh ÷ 1000 = ____ kwh

Four-slice toaster:

____ w × 2.5/60 hr = ____ wh

____ wh × 3 (for 12 slices) = ____ wh

____ wh ÷ 1000 = ____ kwh

(Remember, a kwh is 1000 watts for one hour. Convert watt hours to kwh by dividing by 1000.)

Which method uses the least amount of electricity? What factors are important in deciding whether to buy a two-slice toaster, a four-slice toaster, or a toaster oven? Discuss these questions when data are gathered. Discussion will likely lead to additional comparisions.

If small appliances prepare small quantities of food (such as two slices of toast or two hamburgers) with a small drain on electrical current, should comparative efficiency enter into decisions to buy more small appliances?

Find out how many households there are in your city. If you don't know the exact figure, divide the population of the city by 3.5 and use that figure as the approximate number of household units. How does the number of households relate to peak hours of electrical consumption? When do most families prepare dinner? Could changes of cooking methods reduce peak demands?

CONSERVING LIGHT ENERGY

How much artificial light do we need in the environment? What types of artificial lighting give the most light for the energy consumed? How could we reduce the amount of electricity we use for lighting? The activities below will answer these questions.

Several terms are useful in making observations and doing calculations in this study. Electricity use is figured in terms of watts per hour and in thousands of watts per hour or kilowatt hours. Light bulbs are usually labeled in terms of watts. The number of watts listed on a light bulb does not tell how brightly it will glow or how much light it will give off. The watts tell how much electrical current it draws. A clear 100-watt bulb gives off more light than a frosted 100-watt bulb. A 40-watt fluorescent lamp gives off more light than a 40-watt incandescent bulb. Thus, a 100-watt bulb burning for one hour uses 100 watt hours of electricity. Ten 100-watt bulbs burning for one hour consume one kwh. It is evident that much electrical energy is consumed for the production of light.

Begin by finding out how much electricity is used for lighting your classroom each day, each month, each year. Ask your school custodian the wattage of classroom light bulbs. Next, count the number of bulbs. Finally, find out how many hours per day the lights are on. For example, suppose you have 24 40-watt fluorescent tubes burning seven hours a day in the room. The number of watts per lamp, times the number of units in the room, times the number of hours lit equals the number of watt hours used each day. That figure multiplied by five is the weekly consumption; the weekly figure multiplied by 4.2 is the monthly consumption of electricity for lighting your classroom.

The figures are based on lights staying on all day. Are there times the room is empty? Are lights turned off when the room is not in use? Suppose the classroom is vacated a total of about one-and-one-half hours each day. How much electricity will be saved each month if lights are turned off when the room is empty?

How many classrooms are there in the school building? If these classrooms, like yours, are occupied and empty for similar amounts of time each day, how many kilowatt hours can be saved if lights in your building are turned off when not needed?

How many classrooms are there in your school district? If your classroom is typical of all classrooms in the district, how many kilowatt hours can be saved each month in your district by turning off unnecessary lights? What are some things that could be done to make sure lights are turned off when not needed?

During science class survey all classrooms in your building. Record which rooms are empty but have on lights. Count the number of light bulbs or fluorescent tubes in the room. If each room stood empty for one-half hour, how much electricity could have been saved by turning off all unneeded lights?

ENERGY ESCAPES AS HEAT

Place your hand near a glowing 40- or 60-watt light bulb. Be careful not to touch it. What do you feel? You have just discovered that some electrical energy produces heat instead of light. What type of light source, the incandescent bulb or the fluorescent lamp, produces more heat, and thus is more wasteful?

Find an incandescent bulb and a fluorescent lamp of equal wattage, preferably 20 watts. Next, find two corrugated cardboard boxes of equal dimension, large enough to accommodate the fluorescent lamp. Position the lights, one in each box, so they do not touch any surface. Insert a thermometer into each box so you can read it without removing it, but being careful that the thermometer bulb is not close to the light source. Seal the boxes with masking tape so little air moves into or out of them. Connect the lights to an outlet, record and chart the thermometer readings at five-minute intervals for one hour.

Which type of bulb consistently produces the higher temperature? What may cause variations in temperatures inside the box? What does the comparison of box temperatures tell you? Which type of light source converts more energy to light? Which type converts more energy to heat? Incandescent lights are about five percent or less efficient, and fluorescent lights are about 20 percent efficient.* Based on these investigations, what does efficiency mean?

---

*Fowler, John M. *Energy and the Environment*. New York: McGraw-Hill Book Co., 1975.

Food Labs: An Approach to Science

Bonnie J. Frimpter
Roy E. Doughty

Even the sleepiest, most reticent junior high students participate in science when science means food. Food labs, in which students observe scientific principles through experimentation with food, provide a creative alternative to traditional approaches to junior high science.

Food labs work on a well-known principle: Teenagers love to eat. Conservation of mass fascinates these youngsters when the investigation involves finding the mass of corn before and after popping. Melting points and solubility are interesting when applied to fudge bubbling over a Bunsen burner. In fact, food labs incorporate many of the important elements in good learning situations for early adolescents:

1. Hands-on laboratory activity.
2. The element of anticipation. ("When do we get to make popsicles?")
3. The element of surprise. ("We didn't know this would be fudge!")
4. Sensory involvement in the learning process.
5. Integration of physical science concepts with concepts meaningful and interesting to adolescents.
6. Enforcement of the idea that science concepts are related to the real world.
7. Teacher enthusiasm and interest.
8. Easy recall. ("Remember when we made popcorn? We found that the mass appeared to decrease.")
9. Use of lab equipment.
10. Responsibility for lab safety.

In any learning situation, the attitude of the teacher bears directly on the attitude of the student. When teachers develop activities that reflect creative attitudes toward learning, students respond enthusiastically. Activities take on new significance, memory of experiences is enhanced, and long-term learning is strengthened. Food labs excite both teacher and students. They prove that learning is relevant, interesting, and even fun.

ACTIVITIES

Here are several food labs we have enjoyed. Try them, or devise your own.

- *Popcorn: Variables*. To help students understand the difference between variables and controls, have them alter (by splitting, peeling, or soaking) corn kernels. Ask the students to compare the altered kernels' popping time and appearance after heating against normal kernels.
- *Popcorn: Change in Mass*. The Law of Conservation Mass is a basic component of most physical science courses. After students have done a series of investigations involving this principle, add an investigation involving corn kernels. Students know that the volume of kernels increases after popping. The question is, does the *mass* increase? Finding that the mass apparently decreases sparks curiosity about the relationship between volume and mass.

- *Popsicles: Freezing Points.* From earlier experiments, students know that water freezes at zero degrees Celsius. To find the effect of solutes on the freezing points of solutions, the students place two test tubes into a halite (NaCl) and ice mixture in a beaker. One test tube contains plain water, the other holds water plus Kool-Aid powder and sugar. Monitoring temperatures in both test tubes, students quickly discover a lower freezing point in the Kool-Aid solution than in water.
- *Hard Candy: Dissolving Rates.* To find out if the surface area of a substance affects the rate at which the substance dissolves, give each student three hard candies. The students break one into small pieces, one into large pieces, and leave the last one whole. The candies are dropped simultaneously into cups containing equal amounts of water. Students observe dissolving rates as indicated by the color of the water. They can then relate dissolving rates to the surface areas of the solutes.
- *Coca-Cola: Separating Components.* In this lab, students separate the components of Coca-Cola or other soft drink. The soluble gas can be separated and tested with lime water and with a burning splint. Distillation separates the soft drink into a clear liquid (water) and syrup. Students test the clear liquid for color, taste, acidity, density, boiling point, freezing point, and solubility of other substances in it. The syrup is tested for the same properties and for sugar.
- *Fudge: Melting Points and Solubility.* Introduce this lab without telling students what the results will be. Instead of using a standard fudge recipe, cite procedure, measurements, equipment, and ingredients in scientific terms. As they work, students see connections between familiar experiences (chocolate chips melting and sugar dissolving) and scientific concepts (melting and solubility).

SAFETY

We conduct food labs with an emphasis on safety, adhering strictly to the following procedures:

1. Food labs are introduced as food labs.
2. Lab ware used for food labs is never used for any other type of lab; we label food lab equipment "For Food Only" and store it separately.
3. Resulting food products are placed in disposable containers (paper cups or aluminum foil dishes) before they are eaten (with the consent of the teacher) or thrown away.

These precautions not only protect students, but teach them the importance of lab safety. If appropriate safety procedures cannot be followed in the school's science labs, use the home economics facilities.

Food labs provide unforgettable reinforcement of the physical principles we teach. We also find that students apply the principles they learn to experiences outside the lab, and as a result find science relevant and interesting.

BIBLIOGRAPHY

1. Cobb, Vicki. *Science Experiments You Can Eat.* J.B. Lippincott Co., Philadelphia, PA. 1972.
2. Ennever, Len. "With Objectives In Mind." *Science.* May 1975. New York City.
3. *Early Adolescence: Perspectives and Recommendations.* National Science Foundation. Directorate for Science Education. U.S. Government Printing Office, Washington, DC. 1978.
4. O'Sullivan, Patricia, *et al. Abstracts of Presented Papers.* National Association for Research in Science Teaching (NARST), Columbus, OH. 1979.

Correlation Between Food Labs and Physical Science

Food Labs	Control	Variable	Hypothesis	Law of Conservation of Mass	States of Matter	Change of State	Freezing Point	Melting Point	Boiling Point	Vaporization	Latent Heat	Solvents	Solutes	Solutions	Solubility of Solids	Density	Saturation	Super Saturated	Crystallization	Viscosity	Surface Area	pH Testing	Introduction to Lab Equipment	Introduction: Writing Lab Report	Proper Use of a Lab Burner	Cooling; Water or Ice "Bath"	Thermometer	Data Recording	Graphing	Distillation	Testing Gases	Flow Charts	Lab Safety
Pop Corn: Variables	✓✓	✓✓	✓✓✓																				✓	✓	✓								✓
Pop Corn: Change in Mass			✓✓	✓✓																					✓								✓
Popsicles: Freezing Point	✓✓	✓	✓✓✓			✓✓✓					✓	✓	✓	✓												✓	✓	✓	✓				✓
Hard Candy: Surface Area	✓	✓	✓✓✓									✓	✓	✓	✓						✓					✓	✓	✓	✓				✓
Soft Drink Lab			✓									✓	✓	✓	✓	✓				✓	✓				✓	✓	✓	✓	✓	✓	✓	✓	✓
Fudge: Review Solubility, Freezing, Boiling, Solutions			✓		✓	✓	✓	✓	✓	✓	✓	✓	✓	✓	✓	✓	✓	✓	✓	✓	✓	✓			✓	✓	✓	✓	✓			✓	✓

Physical Science Concepts and Terminology (Control through pH Testing) — *Laboratory Techniques* (Introduction to Lab Equipment through Lab Safety)

Fifteen Simple Discrepant Events That Teach Science Principles and Concepts

Emmett L. Wright

A discrepant event—a phenomenon which occurs that seems to run contrary to our first line of reasoning—is a good device to stimulate interest in learning science concepts and principles. Here is a list of demonstrations of discrepant events which I have found that stimulate the curiosity of students at the secondary school level, and are good, plain fun as well. A brief description of the materials and procedures for doing fifteen of these demonstrations is outlined, along with a short explanation of the concepts and principles involved.

1. CONTRACTING MATTER WITH HEAT

This event provides an exception to the general rule that materials expand when heated.

Materials: Matches, rubber band, weights

Procedure: Suspend the weight by the rubber band. Ask students what will happen if you put a lighted match near the rubber band. Most will say it will stretch more. Yet, rubber actually contracts when heated; the weight will rise as the match heats the rubber band.

2. FIREPROOF PAPER

These events allow you to heat common combustibles without destroying them.

Materials: Matches, paper cup, drinking glass, water, paper clips and burner

Procedure: (1) Wrap the piece of paper around the glass. If you try to light it with a match, it will not ignite because the glass conducts the heat away too rapidly, maintaining the paper below its kindling point. (2) Place the paper cup on the burner and put water in it about 1 cm deep. When the fire is lit, you can bring the water to a boil without burning the cup, the temperature of which remains at 100° C (the boiling point of water), considerably below the kindling point of paper.

3. VITAMIN C TEST

A dramatic, unexpected color change will occur in the presence of Vitamin C.

Materials: Water, cornstarch, iodine, a variety of foods with Vitamin C (orange juice, rose hips, green peppers, etc.), and without Vitamin C (potatoes, nuts, rice, etc.), small beakers or water glasses, Vitamin C tablets

Procedure: Boil a half teaspoon of cornstarch in a little water. Add 1 or 2 drops of iodine and the mixture will turn dark blue or black. Separate the mixture into several containers. Drop a small bit of food into each container. The foods with Vitamin C destroy the iodine starch complex. Following speculation about the common element in the foods which cleared up the solutions, test the solution with Vitamin C. Draw conclusions.

4. HAMMER HEAD

Hitting a person on the head with a hammer can be painless if it's done right.

Materials: Large book (a dictionary works well), hammer, nails, board and a hearty volunteer

Procedure: Place the book on the head of the volunteer. Put the board on top of it and hammer the nails into the board. There is no pain because the force of the blow is distributed throughout the book as well as cushioned by the air trapped between the pages of the book. (To be safe, you do this; don't let students do this to each other.)

5. RISING RICE

This is an event in which a repetitious series of actions is contradicted in the last trial.

Materials: A glass jar full of raw rice, and a table knife

Procedure: Plunge the knife into the jar of rice several times. When the students begin questioning your sanity, jab the knife in once more and slowly lift. The whole jar will be lifted up. The rice packs so tightly that it provides enough friction to lift the jar.

6. SQUEEZING A GLASS BOTTLE

This event calls for good powers of observation and can be used to demonstrate the role of prior assumptions in problem solving.

Materials: Water, dime, and an empty soda bottle

Procedure: Place the dime over the mouth of the bottle. Drop a little water around the edge to seal it. Grasp the bottle with both hands and squeeze. The dime will begin to dance up and down. As the air inside the bottle expands from being warmed by your hands, the dime is lifted to relieve the pressure. The squeezing per se has no effect upon the glass other than raising its temperature.

7. HUFF 'N PUFF

A forceful blast of air will not always move a light object. The activity illustrates Bernoulli's Principle.

Materials: Piece of light cardboard about 5 cm square, straight pin, and thread spool

Procedure: Push the pin through the center of the cardboard. Put the cardboard on the end of the spool with the the pin going into the hole in the spool. The pin keeps the cardboard from going sideways. Hold the spool with the cardboard aimed at the ceiling and blow hard through the other end of the spool. No matter how hard you blow, you cannot blow the cardboard off the spool. A variation of this event for those rooms with air jets in them is to use a thistle tube and a ping pong ball. Place the ball in the mouth of the tube, but not too close. Turn on the air and the ball will blow away. Now place the ball very close to the tube. This time the air will not blow the ball away; instead it holds the ball in place even if the tube is moved around.

8. "IRON" FIGURES

A mysterious figure appears when iron filings are sprinkled onto a piece of cardboard.

Materials: Two sheets of light cardboard, bell wire, iron filings, dry cell, and scotch tape.

Procedure: Cut a simple figure out of a sheet of cardboard. Tape it to another sheet. Tape wire around the edge of the figure and run it to the hidden dry cell. With the figure side down, lay the cardboard on the table. Sprinkle iron filings onto the cardboard and tap it gently. The filings will align themselves along the wire, "drawing" the figure. The current in the wire creates a magnetic field which attracts the filings.

9. CORK IN THE BOTTLE

Try this experiment in negative acceleration.

Materials: Large bottle at least 10 cm across at the bottom, water, string, and corks.

Procedure: Fill the bottle with water. Tie the string to the cork (one that will fit through the mouth of the bottle) and put it into the water. Leave one end of the string hanging out of the mouth. Plug the bottle with another cork so that the string is held fast and the cork in the bottle is able to float free. Hold the bottle upside down and move it to one side at a constant velocity. The cork retains its relative position in the water. Next, accelerate the bottle in the same direction. Instead of retaining the same position or lagging behind the motion of the bottle (as most students will predict), the cork will spring ahead in advance of the motion and maintain the shifted position as long as the bottle experiences the acceleration. This shift is due to the development of a density gradient in the water. The acceleration causes the water on the side of the cork opposite the direction of acceleration to become more dense. This creates an unbalanced force which shifts the cork forward until a new pressure equilibrium point is reached.

10. BLUE BOTTLE

This event encourages students to analyze, predict and evaluate phenomena.

Materials: 250 mL flask with rubber stopper (or bottle with screw-on cap), 10 g table sugar, 125 mL distilled water, 5 drops methylene blue indicator, and 10 g sodium hydroxide ("Drano" could be substituted)

Procedure: Mix the above ingredients in the bottle. There will be blue in the bottle, but upon setting will turn clear. With vigorous shaking, the liquid will return to its blue color. (For safety you do this. Don't let students do it. Take great care to keep the top on when shaking since sodium hydroxide is a strong base and can harm eyes or skin.) Students will be unable to accurately predict, however, the behavior of the liquid when vigorous shaking is continued after the initial changes in color. This system involves oxidation of the sugar by oxygen catalyzed by methylene blue.

11. CORN STARCH IN WATER

This substance exhibits startling properties when mixed with a little water.

Materials: Clear jar, water and corn starch

Procedure: Fill the jar about one-half full with corn starch. Add just enough water to make a thick paste. Have a student slowly push his finger directly into the paste. It will go in easily and fully. Now ask another student to rapidly punch his finger into the beaker. This time there will be high resistance and the finger will not penetrate. The molecular structure of the starch-water combination maintains its structural integrity on impact, but will give easily, under slow but steady pressure.

12. WATERPROOF CHEESECLOTH

Materials: 2 layers of cheesecloth (or 1 file card), 1 widemouth jar, and 1 rubber band

Procedure: Stretch two layers of cheesecloth over the mouth of a jar and hold them in place with a rubber band. Pour water into the jar slowly. Flip the jar over quickly and the water will not come out. Next, punch a small hole in the cheesecloth with the point of a sharp pencil. Water will run out for an instant, then stop. In both cases the surface tension (the strong cohesive force of water molecules) with the aid of atmospheric pressure "seal" the holes.

This demonstration can also be done by placing a file card completely over the mouth of a jar after it has been filled with water. Holding the file card in place, flip the jar over, then let go of the card and it will "stick" to the jar. The water will remain inside the jar. In fact, the card will remain in place as long as the rim of the jar is wet and the card is in direct contact with the entire edge. Illustrated here is the effect of the differential pressures exerted by the atmospheric air (greater upwards on the card) and the smaller pressure exerted downwards by the water or a combination of water and air in the jar.

13. KUNG FU

Materials: A wooden slat, and 2 sheets of newspaper

Procedure: Place a slat of wood on a desk. Spread two pieces of newspaper smoothly over the part of the slat resting on the desk. Make sure the newspaper is flush on the desk with no air gaps. Strike the overhanging piece of slat, and it will snap in half with the paper remaining in place on the table. This demonstrates the tremendous pressure exerted on the newspaper and transmitted to the slat by the atmospheric air, greater than the force striking the slat. This differential pressure effect is only true if no air is permitted under most of the newspaper.

14. "COOKING" BY FREEZING

Materials: One dozen apples, freezing unit, blender, hot plate, and cooking utensils

Procedure: Prepare for the demonstration by placing apples into a freezer. After the apples are thoroughly frozen, let them thaw. Freezing breaks down the cells in the apple just the same as cooking. Prepare another batch of apples by the regular method. Process both batches in a blender. When both are served to the student, they will not be able to tell which was "cooked" by freezing.

15. LIGHT LEAD

You cannot always trust your senses.

Materials: Piece of sponge (about 50 g, cut to size), piece of lead (about 45 g) and an equal arm balance.

Procedure: Prepare a chunk of lead and a piece of sponge where the sponge is slightly heavier than the lead. Give students the chance to compare weights by lifting them. Ask "Which is heavier?" or "How many times heavier is the lead than the sponge?" To most students, the lead will seem heavier. Place the two items on opposite pans of an equal arm balance and have students react.

Art by Lydia Nolan-Davis